# Parsnips in the Snow

## A Bur Oak Original

# Parsnips in the Snow

Talks with

Midwestern

Gardeners

*Jane Anne Staw*

*and*

*Mary Swander*

University of Iowa Press

Iowa City

University of Iowa Press, Iowa City 52242
Copyright © 1990 by the University of Iowa
All rights reserved
Printed in the United States of America
Second printing, 1990

Design by Richard Hendel

Printed on acid-free paper

Library of Congress Cataloging-in-Publication Data
Parsnips in the snow: talks with Midwestern gardeners/Jane Anne Staw
and Mary Swander.—1st ed.
     p.   cm.—(A Bur oak original)
   ISBN 0-87745-269-5 (alk. paper), ISBN 0-87745-279-2 (pbk.: alk.
paper)
   1. Gardening.   2. Gardening—Middle West.   I. Staw, Jane Anne.
II. Swander, Mary.   III. Series.
SB455.P367   1990            89-20439
635'.0977—dc20            CIP

*For Paul Diehl,*

*our teacher,*

*who inspired us*

*to write together*

# Contents

# Acknowledgments

We thank the following friends for their hospitality and enthusiasm in ferreting out the gardeners we interviewed for this book: Caroline Ash, Thomas Fox Averill, Robin Behn, Carl Birkelbach, Nancy Eberhardt, Jeffrey Goudie, Robert Grunst, Duane Hutchinson, Mary McMahon Klotzbach, William Klotzbach, Eva Leo, Monica Leo, Charles Maland, Dorothy Maland, Nancy Klein Maland, Bonnie O'Connell, George O'Connell, Yolanda Ortega, Dixie Peterson, Susan P. Smith, and Marcia Southwick. Thanks, too, to Sheryl Kamps and Carol Palmquist for their secretarial support and to Linda Verrips for her transcriptions, humorous quips, and genius for deciphering our garbled comments on the tapes. We thank Paul Diehl, Ellen Greenblatt, Elizabeth Pelzner, Randall Vandermey, and Sharon Warner for their editorial comments and encouragement. We especially thank Susan Sobel-Feldman for her criticism and feedback. For permission to reprint, we thank the *Northern Review,* where "The Blessing of the Fields" first appeared. For their financial assistance, we thank the National Endowment for the Arts, a federal agency, and Iowa State University. Also, thanks to Jonah Staw for asking good questions, and special thanks to Barry Staw for sharing our vision from the very beginning.

*Sarge, tell them about the parsnips, the parsnips. Tell them about the parsnips.*

*Well, parsnips. You can plant them in the spring—we planted some this spring—and they stay in the ground all winter. Just let the frost come. Then you dig them out the next spring. That way they're tender. Starch turns to sugar within the parsnips, you know.*

*You can also dig them in the fall. That's what I've heard, but we've never tried it. We leave ours in until April, even under the snow. And you'd be surprised how beautiful they are.*

—Marion and Sarge Wendlandt, Iowa City, Iowa

# Introduction

This book began with the voice of Mary Sorensen. One cool evening in late June, we were puttering in the backyard of some friends. They had just moved into a new house that spring, too late for their peas and broccoli, their usual richly composted rows, but in plenty of time for their tomatoes and peppers, their zucchini and cantaloupe to be in abundant bloom. It was twilight, the cicadas tuning up, the fireflies rehearsing for their nine o'clock pyrotechnics, by the time we wandered over to the white picket fence that separated our friends' lot from their neighbor to the west.

In the next yard, roses and geraniums blossomed along the fence. Concentric circles of strawberry plants coiled not far from the lot line. And in the southeast corner of the lawn, three hundred square feet of broccoli, cabbage, tomatoes, peppers, summer squash and cucumbers lined up in straight, clean rows. At the edge of the garden, the tips of her feet touching the grass, a tiny, white-haired woman weeded on her hands and knees. As soon as she saw us, she stood up, tucking a few stray white curls into the net she wore to keep her hair in place.

"My garden's not as good as it usually is. It's been too dry. And the birds came down and stole all my peas."

That was how she began. She didn't introduce herself. Nor did she cross the yard to stand within earshot. And she certainly didn't wait for us to signal our interest or consent. Instead, for the next hour and a half, this tiny woman flitted from her peas to her broccoli, from her summer squash to her tomatoes, introducing us to her garden and, through her garden, to her life. She told us her name was Mary Sorensen only when we were about to leave—long after her voice had bubbled across the yard and over the fence to describe the farm in Johnson County, Iowa, where she had grown up, and even longer after she had reminisced about her husband, a construction engineer with boundless energy and a zeal for gardening.

"Chris just loved to gather things from the garden. I used to say to myself, Oh, I wish he wouldn't plant so much. He had the plot in the yard. And then he cultivated an empty lot up the block. But he never had enough vegetables. And then when Chris died, I kind of surprised myself. I never

*Mary Sorensen*

used to like getting my hands dirty. And now I can't wait to get out into the garden in the spring."

Over the next few weeks, Mary Sorensen's voice remained with us, as did the image of the wrenlike woman, her housedress appropriately splattered with tiny watering cans, who had told us her story one evening while the sun set and the neighborhood quieted down for the night. By the following summer, when we started out in the pickup to search the Midwest for other committed vegetable gardeners, Mary Sorensen had become our muse, her voice and story the inspiration both for this book and for our journey. As the weeks slipped by and we drove north from Iowa into Minnesota and Wisconsin, then south to Illinois, Nebraska, Missouri and Kansas, interviewing gardeners—on farms, in small towns and in cities—Mary's voice multiplied. Across state lines the accents changed, along with the regionalisms of the gardeners' speech. So did the climates and soils, from the blue-black earth of south central Minnesota to the sandy loam of southern Wisconsin. And, of course, the stories themselves varied, no two ever exactly alike. But at the same time that we encountered differences, we perceived similarities, a certain kindredness in themes or personalities, a congruence in lifestyles or emotions.

This book captures these midwestern voices and their stories. The chapters present a series of personality portraits, each one unique and at the same time typical, expressing the committedness and passion shared by vegetable gardeners from Chicago and Omaha to Oronogo, Missouri, and Blue Earth, Minnesota. Some are voices we sought out, encouraged by friends or lured by the gardener's reputation, which in the Midwest can travel far. Other voices, either through luck or happenstance, offered themselves to us. Larry Fischer, a childhood friend of Mary's from her hometown in Manning, Iowa, read in the Iowa State University alumni magazine that we were writing a book on gardening and invited us up to Waseca, Minnesota, where he and his wife, Marian, cultivate five acres of vegetables and flowers, one acre more gorgeous than the other. On that same trip, a customer sipping coffee and eating lemon meringue pie at the Village Inn Cafe in Winnebago, Minnesota, urged us to visit Roy Nelson's garden in Bricelyn, a half-hour up the road. Roy is a retired veterinarian, with an acre of squash and melons out in the country in the middle of the cornfields—in addition to his backyard plot framed with grape arbors and laced with handcrafted birdhouses and feeders. Roy generously gave us a tour of his garden and his melon patch, then when driving back into town, veered off Highway 169 and pulled up in front of Harold Beckman's. Harold, a former manager of the Owatonna canning plant, not only gardens organically in raised beds, but manages his thriving Beckman Sausage Company, founded a few years ago with a recipe that came to him in a dream.

Floyd Brannon required more determined sleuthing on our part. We had noticed his garden on our way to another interview in Galesburg, Illinois. The plot, crammed with tomatoes, beans, cucumbers and okra, stretched an entire block, between an abandoned school on one end and a lopsided frame house on the other. We approached a neighbor running a LawnBoy over his grass and asked him who tilled the plot across the street. "I don't know his name, but he lives down on the corner of Holton. You can't miss his place. It's an old house with a brand-new garage."

Floyd Brannon was not at home that night. But a friend of the family's peddling by on a bicycle led us around the corner to Floyd's daughter's. She had no idea where her father was, either. "But one thing's for sure," she told us. "He'll be up in his garden in the morning. And he'll be there by six."

At five-thirty the next day, we were staked out in front of Floyd's house. Aside from the paperboy pitching Galesburg's *Register Mail* as he wove down the middle of the street, the neighborhood was deserted, the already humid air filled with the twittering of sparrows jumping from the sycamore in Floyd's side yard to a rusty tiller listing next to his sparkling new garage. Behind us, the towers of Butler Manufacturing rose, casting their shadows over the north end of town.

By seven-thirty Floyd had not yet appeared. At eight, just when we had decided to leave, the front door of his sagging bungalow creaked open and Floyd, dressed in slacks and a sportshirt, a Pall Mall dangling from his mouth, ambled out.

"You girls waiting on me?" he asked, stopping at the truck. "I seen you from the window."

Floyd couldn't talk to us that day. The Brannon family, arriving from Oklahoma, Kansas and Illinois, had scheduled a reunion for that evening. And Floyd was off to Flint's Barbecue in Rock Island to pick up the food for the celebration.

"But any other morning, I be in my garden by six o'clock. You can count on it. Today just an exception."

Two weeks later we circled back. And for hours, Floyd added his voice to the other voices resonating in our ears. We had begun our journey in June, and now it was late July. The heat wave and drought had continued, day after day the sun incandescent, the humidity holding, even building, an obstacle which like the sound barrier had to be broken through, not only first thing each morning, but anytime anybody wanted to move at all. Yet throughout the weather our gardeners kept gardening, some rising even earlier than customary, others working later—but all still going about the business of raising vegetables—cultivating, pulling weeds, pinching the suckers off tomatoes, nudging back the squash.

By the time we completed our journey, we had interviewed over fifty gardeners, each of whom had devoted at least three concentrated hours to us, inviting us into their homes, introducing us to their children and grandchildren, exposing their aspirations and their fears. By sharing these deepest and most intimate parts of their lives, they had coalesced into a community for us, their accents and speech, gardening techniques and motivation, lifestyles and dreams, a microcosm of the Midwest we would carry within us forever.

Although many of the interviews themselves do not appear in the following chapters, this book is steeped in the voices of all the gardeners we spoke to during the summer of 1986. And if the actual words of each of these men and women are not imprinted on these pages, the collective spirit of midwestern vegetable gardeners infuses our work, nourishing it the way Roy Nelson's blue-black earth or the Fischers' chicken manure or Grant Cushinberry's hay fertilizes the soil in their vegetable plots. For if there is one lesson our gardeners taught us, it is that without good soil, no matter how you labor, nothing much can grow.

*—Kalona, Iowa*

# 1     The Good Old Days

You know people now say they have hard times. But they don't even know what hard times are. My father went broke three times when we were growing up. One year there was a real bad storm, a hailstorm that crossed our farm. It killed the chickens and the pigs. We just saw them fall over. The hailstones were the size of baseballs. I remember that year Father had two fields of corn. The hail just flattened them right to the ground. After that, my father ended up a carpenter. He had to go to work when his crops failed. But he started up again. And I remember in those days, we didn't have hot weather until August. I mean real hot. And then during the hay making, for three weeks we had maybe a hundred in the shade. My father used to come in from the fields, and his whole shirt was wet with perspiration. He would sit under a shade tree to cool off, and we would fan him.—MARY SORENSEN, *Iowa City, Iowa*

We started the gardens the summer after we moved into this house, didn't we, Sarge?

And I did just what my mother used to do. She started her own plants. And I still do the same, right here in the living room.

Tell them how you do it, Sarge.

You've got to have sun, you know. So we follow it around the house. We keep the seedlings in the kitchen in the morning. They can get good sun there.

Then we carry them in here to the living room and put them right in front of that picture window. There they have sun in the afternoon. The plants grow up pretty quick that way. Of course, you have to watch them all the time. And water them a lot. And then you have to break them in outside in the real sun. But I learned how to do all that from my mother.

—MARION AND SARGE WENDLANDT, *Iowa City, Iowa*

I mostly just garden the way my dad gardened. My dad, he did truck gardening, but we always had a big garden for our own use. My mother canned about everything she could. But what did she used to say? Yes, that's it: "You eat what you can. And what you can't, you can."

—LARRY CASSATT, *Oronogo, Missouri*

# Pawpaws Everywhere

## An Interview with Edith Cone

*I grew up on a sixty-acre produce farm in Mills County, Iowa, called Ferncrest. We mostly grew apples, but also raised plums, peaches, pears, cherries, grapes and strawberries, and a large variety of vegetables. We kept as many as a thousand white Leghorns, which produced eggs. And we milked cows and sold butter. I obtained a B.S. in chemistry and an M.S. in organic chemistry from Iowa State University in 1928. Five days after receiving my degree, I married my husband, a poultry graduate at Iowa State. We ran a poultry-breeding farm near Independence, Iowa, and gardened to produce most of our food. I still garden, even though my husband has died, and am so self-sufficient that I buy nothing at the store but light bulbs and paper towels.*

—Edith Cone, Independence, Iowa

When Edith Cone recalls her childhood, her voice rising into crescendo then falling, she sounds as if she is quoting from the book of *Genesis*: "And the Lord God planted a garden toward Eden in the East." "I was raised on a produce farm, not only garden but orchard as well, in Mills County in the southwest corner of Iowa, along the Missouri River. My father named our place Ferncrest. When I was small, there were wild pawpaws growing everywhere. We had forty acres of orchard—apples, pears, plums, cherries and berries. My father packed apples in wooden barrels, and shipped them by the boxcar load."

Edith left Ferncrest when she was twenty years old. She is now eighty-one, widowed, and living on her own farm ten miles north of Independence, Iowa. Her white salt-box house sits close to Highway 150 with its hum of combines, pickups, tractors and automobiles. But her garden is set back from the road, a half-acre she still maintains herself, lush with zinnias, hollyhocks, marigolds, black-eyed Susans, comfrey, basil, oregano and chives, as well as the more predictable cauliflower, broccoli, peas, beans, beets and corn.

The roots of this garden stretch all the way back to Ferncrest—past Edith's three children, her marriage and the egg farm she and her husband, Floyd, managed for forty years, past her 1928 master's degree in organic chemistry at Iowa State University, to her childhood, when as soon as she could walk, she picked strawberries alongside her father and sat beside him on the buckboard on the road to the Bartlett railroad station with shipments of eggs destined for Council Bluffs.

"I loved my father. He was an inspiration. And that's the way I raised my children, too. I worked at Ferncrest as soon as I could get around, and my children did the same thing with me here. As soon as they had two hands to work and could understand what I was saying. That's the only way to do it. Don't go flying around and do nothing like those city kids."

The first time we saw Edith she was crouched in her broccoli patch, a giant sunflower head drooping above her. She looked like part of the landscape, her head bent to one knee, her gray hair pulled into a tight bun, the dowager's hump on her back in the shadow of the sunflower leaves. Beyond the garden, a cluster of outbuildings, two full henhouses, an old slatted corncrib bursting with cobs, and two forty-cow barns announced the business of everyday farm life. Further off, a pasture sloped toward the horizon,

*Edith Cone*

emerald here, chartreuse there, kelly green in the distance where Edith's Guernsey, Belle, a brown-and-white blur, grazed.

"How about a couple heads of broccoli to take home with you?" Edith's knife was poised to cut across a thick, fibrous stem, the joints and knuckles of her hand knobby with arthritis. The skin on her thin arm was as dry as cornhusks. "You *can* use some broccoli, can't you?" Edith raised her head and widened her ice blue eyes.

From her widow's peak, a streak of black snaked through the gray toward the back of her head and wound into the bun that drew her hair up and away from her oval face, the skin puckered around her mouth and chin, wrinkles scoring her forehead. Edith whacked off three heads of broccoli, then propelled herself up off the ground with her left hand, and hobbled back toward the edge of the garden. The breeze fanned her army shirt and blue bell-bottoms out from her skeletal frame.

"You just stay there and I'll bring it to you. I don't want you stepping on any of my seedlings," Edith yelled, the broccoli dangling from her hand like an old purse. "Now, you eat this raw, just like everything else. Never eat anything cooked, no indeed. I don't roast or cook anything I can eat raw. Not even peanuts."

Edith pointed a crooked finger toward a row in the southwest corner of her garden where the delicate leaves of the peanut plants grew in tangled mounds, the legumes developing several inches below ground. In the fall, about the time of the first frost, Edith digs the peanuts, dries the vines on her clothesline, then shells and eats the nuts. "Folks ask me, 'Do you roast your peanuts?' 'No,' I tell them, 'I eat them raw.'" She also eats her walnuts and sunflower seeds unroasted, stripping the sunflower hulls off with a blunt knife.

Edith dropped the heads of broccoli into a paper bag which she rolled shut and handed to us. When she stood, she barely reached our shoulders. "I eat everything raw," she said, her thin lips drawn taut across her face. "It's very much better for us. Cooking destroys vitamins and enzymes, although minerals are stable and remain unchanged. When you don't cook, you destroy *nothing*. So I start in the spring with dandelions and pick them as soon as they come through. But I don't plant my dandelions. No, I eat them right from the lawn. I do not chemicalize my grass, or anything else for that matter. And that gives me an advantage there. And after the dandelions, I go on to radishes, lettuce, beets, broccoli, cauliflower, cabbage,

comfrey, carrots, apples, peanuts and walnuts. I eat nothing from a bag or a box. When I go to the supermarket, the only thing I buy is white paper towels. Or occasionally a light bulb."

Several gray wisps that had escaped from Edith's bun fluttered at her temples. "You know, even animals, when given a choice, know what's best for them. A friend of mine stored a great deal of food in his garage one year: white rice, degermed cornmeal and white flour, as well as whole corn and whole wheat. And the rats ate every last bit of his whole corn and wheat. But they didn't touch any of the processed stuff. I tell that to everybody to try to convince them that even our four-legged furry friends have more sense than we do when it comes to food."

Self-sufficiency and good nutrition have become more than particular virtues for Edith. She has blended them into a second religion in a life already rich since childhood with French Huguenot Presbyterianism. Her father claimed to be an eighth-generation Presbyterian. Edith's eldest son is a Presbyterian minister. And Edith still drives herself the ten miles to church in Independence on Sundays. In addition, every few years, as part of her Christian commitment, she sponsors a Third World family in Iowa.

One of the people Edith celebrates her hybrid religion with is Brian, an assistant at the First Presbyterian Church in Independence. Often, the hymnals replaced in the pew racks, the collection tray emptied and counted, Brian and his new bride, Becky, accompany Edith home from Sunday services. "Now Becky isn't much of a farm girl, so I give her a book and she stays in the house to read. But Brian likes to work in the garden. He keeps his shoes and jeans here and the first thing we do is tend the hens."

Aside from Brian and her grandchildren, Edith allows no one in her garden. Nor does she permit the cutting of flowers for bouquets, preferring them in their natural state. "They look prettier and last longer outside." In everything she does, Edith is driven by a sense of correctness and order, her days governed by a strict schedule. She rises at five and, at dawn, goes directly to her garden, continuing to work on the farm and in the house until eleven P.M. Everything around the place is tidy. There are no stacks of scrap metal, junk cars or machinery piled under trees. No discarded feed bags or pesticide containers litter the grounds. Even the barnyard is spare. And Edith's garden rows are perfectly straight, the soil so clean and loose that her knees made deep imprints when she lowered herself near a row of Austrian pine seedlings and began digging with her knife.

"A weed! A weed! I spotted a weed!" she shouted, and continued along the row on her hands and knees, stabbing and gouging, stabbing and gouging, puffs of dirt flying up around her face, then drifting back down into the garden as she worked. "You know a little weed gets to be a big weed mighty quick. And I spend quite a lot of my time pulling them out and using them as mulch on the rest of the garden. Since my stomach surgery in 1981, my muscles aren't good. And if I stand for very long, I just get worn out. But I can work on my knees for half a day."

When she reached the end of the row, Edith sliced off a head of cauliflower. "You can eat this raw with yogurt dip. That's the way I feed my company, too." That Sunday Edith had had as guests Dr. Steven Jungst, chair of the Forestry Department of Iowa State University, and his student, a recipient of a scholarship Edith had endowed in memory of her son, Milton, who had been killed in Vietnam. Milton hadn't believed in the war but had been drafted in the last call just as he was about to complete his master's degree in forestry. He was killed his first day of action.

"Milton was over six feet tall and had a very developed physique. So the other Iowa boys got desk jobs, but they sent my *son*, who loved trees, to the front lines."

On the morning of his visit, Dr. Jungst had called to ask if Edith knew a good restaurant in Independence. "I don't eat away unless I have to. Would you like to eat with me?" Edith had asked him. "So we agreed and we had rhubarb, no sweetening. And I had some raspberries, no sweetening. And that made a very tasty dessert. We had asparagus. We had spinach and lettuce. And yogurt. That's the salad dressing, my make, of course. And corn pone. We had potatoes. And beets cooked with garlic and onions. And carrots. I also had meat from my own beef. And I brought in some comfrey. I just received a letter today in which Dr. Jungst told me he'd harvested the last of his peas, and complimented me on the meal. He even liked the comfrey.

"I've told you about comfrey, haven't I? Comfrey's a natural antibiotic. And all my animals are silly about it. Once we started feeding it to the calves, we didn't buy any more medication for newborn cattle ever again. And those calves grew better than any we ever had. At first, I made a tea from several leaves, and believe it or not, those calves took the comfrey tea quicker than they took milk. Now I just grab a big bundle and feed it like hay. They're that silly about it. And I use it for myself, too.

"In the summer, I eat two leaves raw every day. I also dry the leaves and put a leaf or two in every bit of my vegetable cooking. And then if I get a cut, I use comfrey for that, too. Like right here, I have a damaged spot, and I just rub it with the end of the stalk like this. And I've had folks come out from town to get some. One child was attacked by a dog, just all clawed. His parents came and got some comfrey tea. Later, they told me the tea had healed him all up."

Edith led us away from the garden, calling back over her shoulder as she scuttled along, several leaves of comfrey tucked at her side for the hens. When we approached the coop, the cackling exploded from inside, the chickens screeching and flapping, scratching in the dirt. "There on my right, I have my meat chickens, a hundred and fifty of them. And on my left in the chicken coop are my layers. And back there is the post where I hang them up to kill them."

Edith's slaughtering apparatus, a two-by-two nailed across two four-foot stakes, defined the outer limit of the farmyard. On one side sprawled the barns and chicken coops, surrounded by stretches of bare earth punctuated with tufts of crab grass. The air was filled with the high-pitched fussing of the hens. On the other side, Edith's pasture ran to the neighboring farm, a small herd of Guernseys grazing in a hollow to the left. Beyond the pasture, the July corn ripened, its deep green stalks now waist high. Puffs of cumulus clouds drifted across the sky.

"See, I hang the chickens on here by their legs. Then I kill them. I like to take a knife and go right into the brain. That gets them immobile. Next I take off the heads so the blood drains out. Then I have a pail of hot water and get them ready to pluck.

"My husband Floyd was a poultry graduate from Iowa State College. There hasn't been any such thing for years. But poultry raising was a major industry in Iowa in those days. Nearly every farm had chickens. I married Floyd five days after I received my master's. I never had a job because I had a man waiting for me. When we were married, Floyd was managing a small hatchery for A. H. Schwartz. But the next spring Schwartz said he couldn't afford to keep Floyd any longer. 'We'll stay for free,' Floyd told him. And that summer, the two of them, Floyd and Schwartz, went into the hatchery business together.

"Of course, I worked along with them. Floyd and I always worked side by side. We already had a garden then. And we'd hurry up and eat a meal so we could go out on our own time to tend it. At noon. At night. We worked pretty much around the clock, every daylight minute. But we had a garden."

For the next seven years, Edith and Floyd lived on fifty dollars a month. After that, business boomed. With Floyd and Schwartz's hatchery, farmers no longer had to incubate chicken eggs themselves. The business covered thirty acres with ten thousand chickens and five thousand turkeys. The hens were all pedigreed and Edith kept records of their eggs—the texture, the color, the size of the shell, the viability and hatchability.

"By the way, do you have room in your cooler for some eggs?" Edith felt her way into the chicken coop, down the dark, narrow aisle, the air humid with the smell of droppings and hay dust, and bent over a pine egg box. She clutched several recycled egg cartons in the crook of one arm. "I'll give you three dozen. And that's none too many."

Edith twisted around and cocked her head up at us from where she knelt beside the eggs. "I'm going to say this now, and I'll say it again. There's no such thing as an egg being poor food. This is nature's—God's—best production. There's nothing bad about an egg, in spite of all you may hear. Sure, there's cholesterol, but our body produces a lot of that. There's also lecithin in eggs, and in the right proportion the lecithin balances the cholesterol. An egg's the best protein you can eat. I eat twenty-one a week. That makes three a day, two in the morning, and one in my custard at night.

"Nuts and seeds are also some of the best food you can eat. And I raise soybeans for their amino acids. Then mung beans for sprouting. And also garbanzos. And I try to eat a lot of cabbage, red even more than green, because deeply colored plants are better nutritionally than even green ones. They've got more vitamin A.

"I also eat lots of garlic and onions. They're very helpful in keeping blood pressure down. And I eat no white flour and no fat. That's also for my blood pressure." Edith slid the top of the third egg carton down, the Styrofoam squeaking as it caught. Then she rested her hands on the square pine box her husband Floyd had made, the wood darkened and slick, the looped metal handle erect. Thirty-six eggs, some speckled with hen droppings, nestled on the bottom.

"These eggs are especially healthful. I feed my chickens my own formula. There's corn and oats and a vitamin mixture. And I grow all the corn myself. I have five different plantings, and I raise open-pollinated, not the hybrid stuff which can have as much as a third less protein. Also, with hybrids, you can't save your seeds, and I save all my seeds. And I grind all my corn to make meal for corn pone. If you want the recipe, you'll have to go inside."

Dust billowed into the air, trailing a semi that whooshed by on the highway, and Edith lurched in its direction as she approached the side entrance of the house, spine bent, arm crooked at the elbow. Inside her breezeway an old table, its top cluttered with clay pots, a tray and gardening gloves, wobbled as the screen door slammed. A cot hugged the inside wall, a Mexican blanket folded at its foot.

In the kitchen a gleaming woodstove jutted out from one wall, its back capped by two warming ovens. Stainless steel soup and canning cauldrons glinted from the stove top, the drainboards and the long rectangular kitchen table. Next to the sink, a dishtowel hung from the horn of a wooden bull's head the size of a softball, a gift from Edith's daughter. Chairs were tucked in each corner and around the table, emblems of Edith's social side, of her urge to cook, feed and nurture friends and relatives alike.

"Now here's the recipe for corn pone. That's the only thing I use for bread. If I have guests too long, I have some wheat berries in the freezer that I grind. But I principally use corn. I have a field for my cows and me that I harvest by hand in bushelbaskets. And I shell it by hand, although I don't use a couple of rocks to grind it."

To make corn pone, Edith stirs together two cups of ground cornmeal, three tablespoons of safflower oil and two-thirds cup of boiling water. She lets the mixture cool, then forms twelve to fifteen tablespoon-size cakes which she puts in the palm of her hand and imprints with three fingers. She bakes the corn pone for thirty-five to forty minutes at 375 degrees.

"Of course, I bake them in the woodstove. I use that every day of the world even if it's a hundred degrees. I even heat the water on it for washing the cows before milking. I also put my chicken and beef bones in the stove and burn them. Then I put the ash in the garden. That contributes a lot of phosphorus, which is very useful, particularly in the asparagus, raspberries and strawberries."

Functional, spare, almost austere, the living room which opens off the

kitchen reflects another side of Edith. On the day of our visit, religious mottoes and family photos were the only adornments. Under one window, a desk, a half-written letter askew on its surface, looked out onto the side yard. Beside the letter lay a small Bible, its binding unglued, its pages loose. In the middle of the room, an easel displayed a shawl friends had brought Edith from Russia. A gray sofa spanned the length of the picture window facing the highway.

"Some people think my diet is strange, but at Ferncrest we raised all kinds of vegetables most folks didn't know much about. In those days, nobody else produced sweet potatoes. And we even grew various types of beans like the Great Northern. My father had poultry, too, a thousand laying chickens, Leghorns. He shipped the eggs on boxcars up to Council Bluffs. It was only thirty miles away, but he didn't drive the team there."

Edith captured a few stray hairs with a comb she wore at the side of her bun. The room was quiet, the hum of highway noise muffled by the thick walls of the house.

"My father raised everything, and my mother canned. That was our only means of preserving, aside from keeping things raw. We had two very nice caves where we stored food. It was hilly in Mills County, so we could easily dig cellars. One of our caves was cemented inside, and that's where we kept all our canned goods. We put our melons in there, too. We also had a refrigerator that was kept cold with ice. My father would go to the Missouri River and cut thick frozen chunks and store them in sawdust in the icehouse. It kept all summer. We had some neighbors who liked to make ice cream, and he let them use some of our ice once in a while.

"In our cave, we had onions and potatoes and barrels of apples. Not the soft summer apples, but the hard winter ones. They could have been Ben Davis, which you don't know about anymore. Or they could have been Winesaps; those are long keepers. And we kept eggs in that cave, too.

"We worked all summer to fill up those cellars. We weeded. We picked berries. We brought in the vegetables for our use and to sell. My father had many helpers because he had a lot of detailed work to do. Once, when I was very young, I believe it was in 1906, my father had planned for fifty neighbors and their families, in addition to the helpers, to come the very morning a damaging hailstorm arrived. After the storm, there wasn't even a raspberry cane left in the ground. And the leaves and trash mixed with the hail in the ditches and lasted for seven weeks.

"But most summers, there were no disasters. And my sister and I would go out and pick strawberries if it wasn't too wet. And we would pick as soon as day broke, which might be at four-thirty. We got the same rate of pay as the other pickers. And we both went to Iowa State College on our savings. It didn't take much, but on the other hand, when I got to college and worked, I earned thirty-five cents an hour. And it cost twenty-four dollars for a dorm room for the whole quarter, and a similar amount for registration.

"But when I was still at Ferncrest, we got up early in the morning to pick berries, or whatever had to be done. Then we always had to rest some. I was taking piano. My sister took piano, so one would rest and the other would practice. Then we'd change places. I can remember very clearly lying on the floor for an hour, resting, while my sister practiced piano, and vice versa. We played duets together and we generally enjoyed one another.

"Of course, I do have a resentment against her. I was ready for school a year and a half before Nina. But my mother couldn't see little Edith going to the country school alone, three-quarters of a mile away from home. So she kept me back until Nina was able to go. I still think that was the wrong thing to do."

The late afternoon light filtered through the picture window, falling on Edith's head, highlighting her fine bones, her straight nose and jaw,

*Edith Cone*

softly peaked like a freshly laid egg. A few coarse hairs poked out from her chin. Her skin, stretched tight across her nose, was mottled, fair on her cheeks, darker around her temples, with small patches flaking under her eyes. Her hair crowned her head, the white streaks radiant. She looked beautiful.

Suddenly, Edith pivoted toward the picture window. "There's something going on out there. I just know there is." She slid out of her straight-backed chair and pulled the front door open. A current of fresh, warm air wafted into the room. Her Russian shawl flapped against the easel. "Oh, yes. I knew I was right. I'm never wrong. They're beginning construction on that road over there. You live long enough and you know all the sounds.

"Of course, now I've lived so long, I can't work as hard as I used to. But I'm not going to leave this place. People say, 'Why don't you just give it all up and go to town?' I won't. I still bring my daughter in Oklahoma City a great deal of her food. But I don't drive all the way myself anymore. The last trip I made was in December. A member of our church took me and a big load. Sagged the springs in his Japanese station wagon. We took three hundred pounds of beef, thirty chickens. We took corn and beans and potatoes, apples and onions, and much more. In the past, I've taken my daughter as many as forty different items of one kind or another.

"And this spring, my grandson, David, came to visit. He hadn't been to see Grandma in four years. He got here on the nineteenth of May. The next day he went out to the garden. 'Grandma,' he said, 'the strawberries are getting red!' And he was tickled to pieces."

Edith glanced at the clock on the wall and her face contracted, her lips and chin collapsing in a maze of wrinkles. "Last night I was up until one o'clock and this morning I got up at five and started working. But there's still never enough time to get everything done."

She hoisted herself up out of the chair and disappeared, the screen door banging behind her. By the time we caught up with her, Edith had harvested two large zucchini. "Do you want to take these home? If you do, I'll get a sack for you from the loft."

In the barn, Edith seesawed up a ladder to a stack of brown paper bags piled on a high shelf. Then, hanging onto a rung with one hand, she looked down. "You see, I so seldom go to the grocery store that I never have any sacks. People have to bring these to me."

Friends might bring Edith paper bags, but they bring her little else.

Instead, she is the one who shares her bounty with the world. Meat, milk, fruits, vegetables, healing herbs—on a rural route in the middle of Buchanan County, Iowa, just at the bend where the road jogs north toward Oelwein, Edith has created her own Garden of Eden. And there she remains.

"No, I won't give it up. Imagine strawberries by the nineteenth of May. And in Iowa. I refuse to leave. Gardening is going to keep me going. If you sit down and do nothing, what are you going to end up with?"

# Truck Farming Back Then

## An Interview with Joe Kantor

*I was born in Omaha, Nebraska, in 1921, and grew up working on my aunt and uncle's truck farm. From 1942 through 1945, I served in the U.S. Army, the infantry, and saw combat in Germany and France. I was supposed to go to the Pacific, but the day I arrived back in the United States on a furlough, they dropped the atomic bomb. I came back to Omaha and worked in the Armour meat-packing plant, then, in 1951 until retirement, for the U.S. Post Office. First I was a clerk on the mail trains. Then, when they faded that out, I carried mail. I've gardened all the time, enough to feed my family and sell to customers along my mail route.*

*—Joe Kantor, Omaha, Nebraska*

"Why don't you girls interview a professional gardener? Not someone like me who don't know nothing." Joe Kantor whisked us into the kitchen and offered us seats at the red formica table pushed up against a wall. Then, without waiting for an answer, he nodded, lifting his USA TODAY seed cap off by the bill and smoothing his thinning white hair. "Hot out there, ain't it! Yip. It's hot. But we went central three years ago. My wife, she won't do without air conditioning. 'Course, I get cold feet just going into the bathroom." Joe gave three short laughs, then narrowed his eyes, folding his thick hands on the table.

Behind his head on the wall, a square tile plaque implored, "Oh, Lord, let my words be tender and gracious. For tomorrow I may have to eat them." Next to the plaque a plastic butterfly poised for takeoff, and above the butterfly, a gnome, his hands on his hips, peered across the room. Figures of Bambi, more butterflies, and signs exhorting us to "SMILE" decorated other walls, along with a hooked rug covered in plastic. A picture of Jesus glowed from the refrigerator door. "Like I said, why don't you two interview a professional gardener?" Joe repeated.

We explained that we weren't after professional instruction, but the stories and wisdom of people who gardened for the love of it. And we had heard through a friend, who bought vegetables from him, that Joe was a good talker. We didn't tell him that our friend considered Joe a dying breed. For Joe, a retired mail carrier who not only gardens prodigiously but thinks and talks about gardening constantly, change, progress, modernization all translate into loss.

"Well, I don't even have my old garden any more. My cousin, he gave me an acre and a half a long time ago. Wanted me to keep the weeds down. But that's up for sale now, so I didn't want to plant it. You know, if it sold, I'd lose all my work. Now I got about three-quarters of an acre. But you should've seen the gardens back before the war, when my aunt and uncle had a truck farm right here in South Omaha. Yip. They used to have forty acres. Down there by Builders' Supply they had seventeen. And then some more down near Unit Step Company. And more down by the old Cart Ranch. It was kind of piecemeal, but all that was in truck gardening. Of course, that's all gone now. With the population increase and the modern care, why, it's altogether different. Gardening was done by horses in those days. And that's really the only way to do it. Now there's no horses so you

*Joe Kantor and his grandson, Aaron*

have to rely on modern equipment. Yip. They got machines for plowing and cultivating. And they got them for planting, too. Why, for all I know, they got something that's completely automatic, now, some kind of robot or something to do your gardening."

Joe laughed three times again and clasped his hands behind the chair. White chest hair sprouted from the V-neck of the T-shirt he wore underneath a blue-and-green plaid sports shirt. A quietly intense man, Joe speaks in bursts, his voice rising and projecting at the ends of sentences or ideas, then falling, gathering volume, and rising once again. For him, talking is a way of thinking out loud, a way of reflecting on his current life, renewing dialogues with family and friends—either dead or simply momentarily absent—and, perhaps most of all, a way of resurrecting his past.

"Yip. There were a lot of truck farms around here in those days. Here in South Omaha, and in East Omaha and along the airfield. They used to have the old market down there, too. Why, we'd go down at four o'clock in the morning with our produce. But see, when the market collapsed, my cousin had to pedal to the grocery stores. And then even to the houses. Yip," Joe nodded, agreeing with himself.

"Then agriculture changed and we lost all the truck farmers. They had to come into the city and get work. In those days it was nothing at all to pick two, three, four hundred baskets of cucumbers a day. Four hundred baskets tomatoes. And my aunt and uncle, they planted maybe a hundred bushels of potatoes. Five, ten acres of sweet corn. And an acre or two of onions. And you had to weed those, you know. And cantaloupe, three or four acres. But you can't hardly raise that stuff here anymore."

We knew what Joe was talking about. Earlier in the day, after visiting the community gardens at Boys' Town, three acres divided into eighty plots and set aside for the public to cultivate, we had headed for Joe's, intending to scout out any interesting gardens along the way. But even after we had turned south off Interstate 80, leaving the most densely populated areas of Omaha behind, we could find no garden plots among the jigsaw of neighborhoods dense with bungalows and ranch-style homes, their tiny lots defined by narrow strips of brittle grass. By the time Joe's place came into sight, the modest one- and two-story houses were giving way to the low-slung concrete-block structures of light industry, and we had begun to wonder whether the friend who had told us that Joe cultivated almost an acre had been mistaken.

"I don't know if it's the chemicals in the air or what, but you can't grow nothing around here anymore." Joe lifted his seed cap and smoothed down his hair again. "A lot of traffic goes by down there on that road where we used to have the truck farm. And anyway, there's not much land left, you know. I had a cousin who had a tavern there. He sold it to some people. Investors. Yip. You couldn't buy no ground for agriculture now. You'd go broke. It goes for ten thousand bucks an acre around here. There's an acre out there on 105th and L, they want 315 thousand. When I come back from the war it was still twenty-two dollars an acre. You could have bought anything you wanted back then.

"But the war, that changed everything. It changed the whole world. Do you know, there's even more weeds since the war. And I don't even know half of them myself. But I know we never had musk thistle here before. You know, them thistles with the big purple flowers. I suppose they came in by truck. Or air. Who knows. I mean, Americans travel everywhere, don't they? Yip. I hear they control the thistles out of state. But I know Douglas County's full of them. I got some right now out in my yard. And you go down there about a mile south, and you'll find property there that's nothing but a sea of purple flowers.

"Yip. And we've also got this other new weed. Some kind of creeping thing with white flowers. And boy, are they hard to eradicate." Joe raised his eyebrows and frowned, accentuating the deep creases running up from his mouth to his eyes and forehead. His expression froze, and for a moment his face looked like a mask, an exaggeration of its animated self, the fleshy tip of his long nose, bulbous, the solid lines of his chin, squared off, and the slight swellings under his eyes, bags.

"Now we used to have ironweed. And ragweed. And hempweed. You know, marijuana. Yip. Big carloads of it. That's why we used to have so many turtledoves. They feasted on the hempweed seed. Oh, man, they loved that! They'd go down the fields in August and you'd see them flying every which way. They were dizzy. Of course, we'd never heard of smoking the stuff back then. But the Papio—that's short for the Papillion, the creek that runs through here—used to be plumb full of hempweed."

Joe's grandson, who had been watching television with his younger sister in a room off the kitchen, sneaked into the refrigerator for a Coke. Chuckling, Joe followed the boy out of the room with his eyes, then explained that he and his wife, Margarita, took care of their son's children during the day while their parents worked, but that the family would soon be taking a trip out to Seattle to visit relatives. "Give the kids something to do, you know. Let them see a different part of the country.

"But I don't know, the kids today, they're not like we used to be. Can't get no real work out of them. I got four children. And not one of them knows anything about planting. They're not even interested. Not like me. Boy, I used to work hard on my aunt and uncle's farm. Planting. Weeding. Cultivating—on my knees! And I worked with the horse a lot. And we'd plant the seeds with a driller. You know, we used to mark the rows. Not like they do today. When my aunt and uncle were making their living from gardening, they were gonna try to get all they could in the space they had. Just like a developer building houses today. Yip. Did you know, these fellows can fit fifteen houses to an acre?"

Joe removed his cap again, smoothing back his hair, wet with perspiration despite the central air conditioning. The back door whooshed open, and a young man, robust, and sweaty from the 90 percent humidity outdoors, sauntered in and headed straight for the sink for some water. He drank long, leaving the faucet running between glasses, a hard, steady stream. Then he flicked his head in our direction and disappeared into the TV room.

"That's my youngest. Any minute now, you'll see his girlfriend come prancing in here after him. That's all he's interested in. Girls! By the time I was his age, eighteen, I don't know how many bushels of vegetables I had picked. And then when I came back from the war, I was interested in gardening, too. But if you didn't have no money then, you couldn't buy nothing. Everything started going on up, you know. If you were a gambler and put your money in something and it went up, why, you could start that way. But I never could get on my feet.

"Now, my folks had a garden. But that was enough for my dad to tend to. You know, when you're grown up, you're out of the picture. Then, like I told you, when my aunt and uncle died about fifteen, twenty years ago, my cousin (he was a superintendent down at Crown Products, and worked sixteen hours a day), he wanted me to plant a garden and keep the weeds down on the property. But like I said, I don't have that garden anymore. And now the one I've got is full of weeds."

It had been a wet spring. One day it had rained six inches. Forced to wait until the soil dried out, Joe hadn't been able to garden for ten days after that. By then, the weeds had the upper hand. "Not only that, but this heavy soil we got here, when it finally dries out, it gets like concrete." Joe laughed his three laughs. Then, unable to remain in the present, he was back to lamenting the past, when horses didn't pack down the soil the way tractors now do, and farmers used manure instead of commercial fertilizers, which, "who knows, are maybe poisoning us all.

"Like I already said, you can't hardly raise cantaloupes here anymore. Same with tomatoes. And I'm having an awful time with my peppers. I don't know what's hit them. The leaves is all brown and falling off. A lot of the chemicals they used before, I don't think they hurt anybody. But you can't get them no more. You know, they used Paris Green for potatoes. And for tomato plants, Zineb. These chemicals the farmers use for weed control now, they're powerful. They're killing off the fish and contaminating the wildlife. There's hardly any pheasants left anymore. 'Course, there's no cover for them anyway 'cause of all that big equipment they got now."

Joe sat up in his chair, squaring his feet on the linoleum as if working to conjure the world that, as a kid growing up in the 1930s on Omaha's south side, he knew as real: the sprawl of truck farms, the stink of manure, the soft thud of horses' hooves on the earth, the sight of men, women and children bent over the tomatoes, the beans and cucumbers, the broccoli and cabbage, their necks to the sun.

"Yip. Just the other day, I was down at my cousin's farm at Table Rock and he said there's a guy who's got a twenty-four-row corn planter. Thirty-five bushels of corn fit in that machine. And twenty-four rows at a time. Yip. I think he farms six thousand acres. And that's the reason those farmers are hollering. They got too much stuff. They can't get rid of it.

"If you ask me, they should go back to the horse and wagon and the two-row planter. But if he's gonna do that, the farmer's got to stay out there eight, ten hours a day, too. Not half a day, like they do now, then come into town looking to invest their money in something. Yip. You gotta admit that the country's greedy now. They're not satisfied with forty thousand, fifty thousand. They want a hundred thousand. Some guy's got a million; he wants two. And the thing of it is, you only got it for so long. Then you have to give it back!"

It was four-forty-five and Joe's wife slipped into the tiny kitchen to begin preparing hot dogs for the grandchildren's dinner. She removed the plastic packaging and plopped the meat into a pot of water. Joe introduced us, then turned back to the table.

"Well, I'm not saying there's anything wrong with trying to save a buck, you know. Yip. Like with my seeds, the first thing I do each year is put my order in to Colorado. Well, we used to get them from Forbes in New Jersey. But that was years ago. I suppose they're gone now. After the war, they started selling bluegrass. You know, sod. Everybody was building homes. So there was more money in that. But back in the thirties, Forbes used to have a traveling salesman and they came to this part of the country. Yip. Now I get my seeds from Burrell, and let me tell you, it's a lot cheaper. You can buy bulk. You know, they got cantaloupe seeds in hundred-pound sacks. Around here you can't hardly buy bulk no more. There used to be an old hardware store down in South Omaha. You could go down there and get a pound of sweet corn. Now you gotta pay ten seeds for a dollar. Yip."

Joe likes to gain time as well as save money. To prolong the growing season, he starts his own seedlings and hardens them off in his cold frame. By about the fifteenth of May, the seedlings are usually mature enough to be transported to his garden down the road. For the transplanting, Joe chooses a cloudy day, when the sun's rays will not put the plants into shock. Too much sun burns the tender leaves, setting growth back for several weeks.

" 'Course, this year after the blizzard, you couldn't catch any cloudy days. I was waiting to put in my cabbage plants, and it was almost 85 and 90 all the time. Yip. The weather was really something this year. Why, this guy down the road here"—Joe flipped his thumb in the direction of the four-lane highway in front of his house—"he said he planted sweet corn the day before the blizzard. First time he ever had sweet corn in June. But the early varieties, I never did like. They got short heads, you know."

A curl of steam rose from the pot bubbling on the stove, the smell of hot dogs wafting through the kitchen and into the TV room, attracting the children. Both Joe's grandson and granddaughter appeared this time, eying us shyly, then scampering across the room to where their grandmother stood at the sink. A doll with a large dial protruding from its back dangled from the granddaughter's arms. "That doll over there can do everything—walk, talk, cry, even suck," Joe laughed. "See, our kids is al-

ready playing with robots!" Then, before the children could take their plates into the TV room, Joe was talking again, leaning back in his seat, his chest out, arms roped around the chair back.

"Yeah, I don't like that early corn. But unless it's damp all the time, it's better to get most things in early. You know, carrots and onions, you should plant whenever the ground is workable. And the same thing with beets. Cold weather never hurt anything. And something like potatoes, they don't do no good here after the Fourth of July. Now in the West, out there by Wyoming, they raise potatoes and they harvest them in the fall. But of course, that's sandy soil and they irrigate. And that's a long ways out there. Scottsbluff. West Nebraska. It's five hundred miles across the state, you know.

"Like I said, different parts of the state get different weather. I have a cousin at Table Rock, and they hardly get half the rain we get. It's kind of a dry pocket there. And Central City used to be wet, and now it's gone dry. And around here, boy, do we get tornadoes! 'Course, they blow the sirens after the storm has passed. I was here one night in June, and they blew that siren. Somebody spotted a cloud floating down over here at 120th and Q, so they started blowing. And a half-hour later, they blew again. But the storm was already gone. Yip. And we got one of them sirens up here at St. Joe High. One of my friends, he went to a wedding in the Livestock Exchange Building, and they made them go down into the basement twice. They was on the tenth floor, and they wouldn't let them ride the elevator. They had to walk down the steps. They got all wore out," Joe laughed. "Yip. I'm setting here when the siren's blowing, and there's people going up the road at seventy miles an hour. I says, More of them get killed in auto accidents than in the storm itself."

Joe's grandchildren scrambled back into the kitchen for seconds on potato chips. Less shy this time, they stopped at the table and giggled at us. They were both fawnlike, with wispy hair and faded freckles and Joe's large brown eyes. "Go on," Joe waved them away and laughed, his eyes dancing, "we're making history here!"

By now Joe had overcome any qualms about talking with us. He was more confident of himself and his expertise, more anchored in the solidity of a past where the scale of life was human and a man's relationship to the earth could be translated directly through his hands—his own temper and a team of horses the largest forces he was called upon to control.

"Yeah, the weather didn't cooperate this year, but I did get a tip from Arnold Peterson, you know, the radio announcer. He's got some special way of putting his tomatoes in the ground. I tried it, and it works, especially if you got the big, long stems. You know, sometimes you get them from the nursery and they're almost a foot long. When that happens, you just lay them down and cover them with soil so they can root all along the stem. And then you let them vine. 'Course, I don't like to buy nothing from the nurseries. You never know what you're gonna get. I got some tomatoes out here. Thought they were regular, and they turned out to be cherries. Then, the seed companies aren't no good, either. Back in March, I bought a few seeds from one of them, but they didn't come up. And my daughter-in-law, she planted some flower seeds and she says they didn't come up. See, big conglomerates own all the seed companies now. And they all went to the hybrids. Young people buy a package and if they don't come up, they throw it away and then forget about it. You know, they say, 'The heck with it!'

"'Course, once the stuff comes up, there's no guarantee. Like with peppers, you only rarely get your maximum crop. I don't know, but it's hard to get it just right. Like here, 85 to 90 degree temperatures burn the blossoms right off. I was over there in my garden the other day, and you just touch the plant and there go the blossoms.

"But I know a fella down there in South Omaha, he plants President tomatoes. He's got them staked on hog wire. Three or four bushels of tomatoes on them. Yip. Right off the Kennedy Expressway. And he's got beautiful pepper plants, too. I said to him, 'All those automobiles rolling through here and all the chemicals from the cars, how you grow anything?' And he says, 'I don't even spray them. No bugs!'" Joe let his jaw drop and rolled his eyes. "Here, we got a million and one bugs today. We never used to have the bean beetle before the war. When the beans come up now, they're just full of holes. Why, those beetles are punching them like nobody's business. And they set them back. Now my cousin, he says, 'Just forget about them. The bugs gotta eat, too.'

"And cucumbers can be a problem. If you don't get out and tend your vines, you'd lose all of them to bugs, too. In the olden days, they just used wood ashes and lime to chase the beetles away. You know, they made a dust for the leaves. I suppose half and half. Then you put the dust in a blower and went down the rows and cranked it as you walked.

"But two years ago, boy, did I have great cucumbers. I think they were Marketeers. They was this big around. Yip. They was so big they wouldn't even fit in a market basket. Of course, you don't see none of those anymore. And if you wanted to buy one, it would cost you a dollar and a half. They used to be two, three cents apiece before the war. Yip. Now anytime you see anybody advertising vegetables, they say to bring your own container!"

A white toy poodle suddenly yapped its way into the kitchen, its nails clicking on the linoleum. "That's Muffin," Joe laughed. "She won't hurt you. . . . Well, this year, I guess, my cucumbers ain't too bad, either. My daughter-in-law canned sixty or sixty-five quarts already. I sold 150, 200 pounds of picklings. Yip. When I was delivering mail, I picked up a few customers. Half the price of what they sell for in the stores. Trouble is, I don't think there's hardly anybody canning no more. The young people all both work, and they don't want to mess with the cucumbers. They make enough money to buy them in the jars."

As he talked, Joe walked over to the back door and hoisted up a plastic bucket of freshly picked vegetables: beefsteak tomatoes, four-lobed green peppers, crescents of light from the fluorescent ceiling fixture reflecting off their flesh, zucchini and odd-shaped pickling cucumbers, their skins ridged and warty. Joe fingered the stem of a tomato, releasing its mintyness into the air.

"Yip. I guess my garden wasn't too bad this year after all. I even gave some things for my daughter-in-law to sell. Traffic's too heavy here. And I don't got enough to put out a sign. You know, you only got a handful. But I said to my son's wife, 'Why don't you put a sign up and buy the kids some clothes or something?' 'Course, they trust people up there. They put a sign out and you just put your coins in the box. If I did that here, they'd probably steal it. Naw, I don't put my trust in nobody anymore. This is a different world. Well, I guess farmers is still like that. I got a cousin, and my grandson and I went fishing over at his place the other night. We just walked right in the front door, and my grandson, he asked me, 'Don't they lock the doors here?'

"Yeah, things has changed. I lock my doors. And I got some modern equipment for my garden, too. I even got a Troy with back tines. 'Course, I also got a hand cultivator. And a wheel hoe. You know, you go down the onion rows and cut the weeds off with the blade. And then I got a hand hoe. But you gotta remember with a hand hoe to get underneath the soil to the root. Otherwise, them weeds will send up new shoots before you can turn around. Oh, and I got a little Mantis, too. I thought it would be ideal for going down onion rows. But let me tell you, it ain't worth a nickel." Joe scrunched up his face, swatting his hand through the air.

"Last June my buddy down here in Bellevue tells me, 'I saw a guy with a little machine, he was really going.' So I says, 'Well, I'm gonna order it, then.' And I paid $258 for that thing. But see, you gotta control the speed by your thumb. And if you get into hard ground, that thing jumps up and down, just like some kangaroo. Yip. I wouldn't give you a nickel for it myself. I'd rather use my hand hoe. Yip. I know a fellow up the hill, he uses his posthole digger to plant his tomatoes. And he told me he knows some guy that always plants his tomatoes *below* the ground. Real early. Says they never freeze. And then he told me, 'Put a little Epsom salt around the roots.' I never tried it. But he says he never failed in all the years. He even told some doctor and now the doctor does the same thing!"

At five-fifteen, Joe's oldest son, finished with work for the day, arrived. This son was tall and thin, a basketball player, judging from his muscular calves and thighs. Hearing him arrive, the children flew out of the TV room and into his arms, the girl first, the boy after. Then the three of them slipped out the door and into the late afternoon August heat.

We wondered if we should leave. It was dinnertime, and we had a three-hour drive home from Omaha to Ames, Iowa. But Joe was finally where he most wanted to be: in his garden—not his current plot, too new to have seeped into his pores and mixed with his blood, but his first, his lifetime garden, the last vestige of his aunt and uncle's forty-acre truck farm, now waiting to be sold.

"Yip. When I garden I do a lot of other things, too, besides cultivate. Like with my corn, I hill it up. You know, throw dirt up against the plants. 'Course, now a lot of farmers, they don't till their corn anymore. There's all that no-till in modern farming. They just swish through the corn once cultivating, and that's it. Well, they can do that because that hybrid, it shoots different kinds of roots. Yip. I seen it. Looks just like your fruit pickers. You know, them metal baskets. Like a crawdad. So, the farmers till once and that's it. Now with my corn, you gotta keep tilling to get the soil up around the stalk. Else, you get a storm and it'll mow that corn down.

"And I do the same with beans. And when it rains, the water drips down off the leaves and along the row. It's a kind of irrigation. All the guys used to do that. And with cantaloupe, you gotta make a ridge before they start to vine out. Otherwise, the melons rot. One year I had cantaloupe, and I planted them a little too close, I guess, and they all got intertwined. And when they set on, you couldn't find the cantaloupes in there. But you could smell them cooking underneath those leaves."

Joe stood up, the tails of his shirt falling down over his hip, and asked if we wanted to drive over to his garden. "You know, when we moved in, there were no other houses around. I had a pretty big garden right here, tomatoes and green beans all the way from the street to the fence line. Now there's that house next door."

Outside, Joe pointed to the traffic on South 60th Street. It was rush hour and cars raced beside the semis churning along after a day of transporting materials to the new interstate, the city landfill or scattered construction sites in downtown Omaha.

"On the road out front, they run over you now. It used to be a nice slow street. Then they paved it into a four-lane about eight years ago. Big trucks running over it all the time. I guess it's like that with everything these days.

"In old Omaha, they tore up all the buildings and they put new ones in. And they say in New York now, after twelve years you can tear anything down. Did you see that fella bought four acres and paid 455 million? Highest price paid ever in the history of the country. And there's a building forty stories high, but it's thirty years old, so they're gonna tear it down. Mega-buildings, they call them now. Gonna build a 150-story-high building there." Joe laughed his triple laugh, his eyes trotting from one of us to the other. "Well, everybody wants to try to get to heaven some way, I guess."

Still laughing, Joe ushered us into his station wagon. His garden tools were all laid out in the cargo area on an old rag rug, and several plastic buckets were stacked on the floor. Newspapers covered the front and rear seats. "Yip," he said, stopping at the end of his drive to wait for a break in the traffic. "Everybody wants to get to heaven. And I'll tell you one thing. You come in this world with nothing and you go out with nothing. Yip. I see them dying every day. All different kind of ages. My hardware man, he was fifty years old. They buried him last week. He was living by himself. Got divorced and he got to drinking heavy. That kills a lot of them today. Yip. And I saw another guy the other day. He told me my supervisor from at the post office was in bad shape. 'What's the matter with him?' I asked. 'Oh,' says the guy, 'he's getting Parkinson's disease.'"

We stopped for a light, and Joe pointed to some land on the right. "See that forty acres over there? Cleanup man in the packing house, he bought it for ten thousand, and two years later, sold it for twenty-eight. And then they were gonna build a mattress factory, but I think the railroad didn't want to put a spur in there. So they sold it to some Oklahoma outfit for 120 thousand. And that's the way things turned out."

We rounded the corner and drove past a small white frame house surrounded by industrial buildings. Clumps of dried-out crab grass poked up here and there through the caked soil. "That was my aunt and uncle's place. They owned all of this. Right alongside here is where they always had the cantaloupes. And over there, where the factory is, they had sweet corn. I carried that stuff out of there with water up to my hips. And over here, where all the buildings are, was all truck farm. A dollar and a quarter a day for ten hours. That was back in the late twenties. All the kids from South Omaha would come out and work."

Joe slowed down alongside a large white building. A bank of concrete steps led to rust-colored double entrance doors. "And this over here used to be corn." He pointed to the other side of the road. "Now it's landfill. They're gonna put in a softball field, a soccer field, and I don't know what all, when they finally get it filled up. You don't realize how much garbage is in the city. You know, we didn't even have pickup here before the war.

And now people just throw everything away. Televisions, washing machines, tree branches, curtains, you name it. You should see them lined up to get rid of the stuff."

Joe turned into a long drive and came to a stop near the end.

"This here's my garden, but like I said, it's no good this year."

We peered out the windows to get our bearings, following the rows of beans and potatoes, beets and cabbage to the barn at one end, and beyond that to the field of sweet corn Joe had told us about. Across the street from the garden, a deserted Funland amusement park steamed in the heat. On the other side, American Concrete Company mixers churned.

"Yip, this garden's no good this year. Full of weeds to begin with, and then we had all that rain. Just look how poor my onions are. And my beets look lousy, too. Yip. I'm almost embarrassed to show this place to you. But you know, I look at life a little differently now. It's full of stress. You don't know if you're gonna have your job from one day to the other. Yip. Look at our meat industry. We had the biggest livestock center here in the whole world. And look what happened. And now the post office wants to put in all part-time fellas. Two different tiers. They'll get rid of all the thirty-, thirty-five-year guys 'cause they're too high paid. 'Course, I don't have to worry. I'm already in the fourth quarter. Almost seventy years old. But you know something. I wouldn't know what to do with myself if I quit gardening. You have no problems when you're out there in the field. You don't think about nothing. All I'm interested in is getting the weeds out."

# Piccalilli and Dog Days

## An Interview with Dixie Peterson

*I've spent my whole life near the little town of Nashville, Missouri, and as a small child, I always had my own garden on my parents' truck farm. As I grew up, I worked along with my family raising vegetables, and made my income that way as a teenager. Now I am a farm wife and the mother of five children. My husband, Bob, and I farm organically, as well as raise an organic garden, because I suffer from a chemically induced condition called ecological illness. I am also a freelance writer with several articles to my credit. And I'm now busy at work on a book.*

—Dixie Peterson, Oronogo, Missouri

Jessica Lange could star in a movie featuring Dixie Peterson's life. Six years ago, Dixie lived just the way she had always dreamed of as a girl growing up in the rural town of Nashville, Missouri. She was an active farm wife, with a doting husband and five children, the three youngest boys strapping blonds destined to star on the football team and help their father on the family's six hundred acres. She also had solid ties to the community, active in the Farm Extension Women's Club, the 4-H, and the Boy Scouts of America. She was affiliated with Christ's Church of Oronogo, where she participated in the Women's Weekly Home Bible Study Group and led youth group meetings. And she had a close relationship to God. As an emblem of all of Dixie's hopes and dreams, the Petersons' brand-new brick ranch house, with wall-to-wall carpeting and an all-electric kitchen, stretched across a rise close to the road at the edge of their fields.

Then Dixie became ill. Because of over-exposure to chemicals, particularly the herbicides and pesticides used on the surrounding farms, Dixie's immune system began to malfunction, causing her to experience severe reactions to most of the substances of daily life. Automobile exhaust, perfumes, polyester fabrics suddenly provoked acute symptoms ranging from vertigo to cardiac arrest. To save her life, Dixie had to move out of her new home and cloister the family down the road in a 120-year-old farmhouse, stripped of most remnants of the modern world, its walls papered with foil to prevent outside contaminants from sifting in. She also had to begin growing and raising all of her own food.

"We lived in a land of plenty, but I had nothing to eat. Everything around me was contaminated. But growing my own food wasn't that hard. I'd always had big gardens. The hardest was leaving our new home. And now every time I drive by and see it looking so beautiful, I feel like crying."

The night we visited Dixie, it was raining hard, a gusting rain. We turned off Highway 171 onto Rural Route 1, outside Oronogo in southwest Missouri, and except for our headlights the night was black, with no houses in sight. Feeling our way along the narrow road, we rounded a sharp curve. The truck heaved to the right, ditch grass switched against the cab and, suddenly ahead of us, framed in darkness, a bank of four windows glowed with light. A few seconds later, three dogs barked. Caught in our headlights, they were lined up along the edge of a drive, their eyes six specks of yellow, their bodies outlined in a luminous mist.

*Dixie Peterson*

Dixie was waiting for us outside, her foot propped against the wide trunk of an elm, the windows of the old farmhouse behind her, two stories, the top dark, the ground floor lit—mud room, kitchen, den and living room. Rain streamed down Dixie's face, from the top of her head to her cheeks and off her chin.

Inside, Dixie grabbed a towel from the mud room, then burst into the kitchen. Dabbing at her neck-length hair, which was plastered to her head, her bangs slick and cut straight across just above her eyebrows, she introduced us to her family: her husband, Bob, her son Travis, and the twins, Tron and Troy. "You can tell the twins apart by the names on their belt buckles. All three boys are in high school now. And Bob, why he'll never grow up."

A few minutes later, Bob disappeared upstairs to bed, and the boys settled in front of the TV in the next room. Dixie continued to towel her hair, the legs of her one-piece yellow jumpsuit rising and falling with the pumping of her arms. Except for her crow's-feet, Dixie looked girlish. The seventeen-year-old high school senior Bob had married twenty-five years earlier still hovered on her face, her eyes avid, a smile flickering on her lips.

"We was just doing some canning. Because of my illness, we have to put up most of our food. This year we've already canned two hundred quarts of tomatoes. And all together, we figured that we put up two thousand quarts of fruits and vegetables, frozen and canned, each year."

More than in any ordinary household, the kitchen is the hub in the Petersons'. Not only does Dixie prepare three farm meals a day on the restaurant-sized electric range, she roasts, dries, freezes, pickles and cans constantly. That night, clumps of Mason jars brimming with tomato sauce, juice and puree collected on the stove and large kitchen table and lined up three deep, nearing the ceiling, on top of the cupboards. As the jars cooled, the burnt red of the pulp glistened from behind the moisture condensing on the glass. The air was humid with a hint of the tomatoes' acidity.

"Now, with my illness, I can't eat commercial food and I'm forced to do all this preserving. But I've loved canning ever since I was a little girl. We used to can so much. Mom did, that is. Hundreds and hundreds of jars. And when I was very little, we had no electricity. Can you imagine in a hundred and ten heat having that woodstove going in the house? Mom used a water-backed canner because there were no pressure canners yet.

And food that was low in acid had to be canned three, four hours. We even canned meats back then. But don't try to do that anymore. Now the composition that they make the lids from is not as good, and so the jars won't work at all for meats.

"Yes, Mama, she canned all day long. But do you know, she would still make the time to take us kids swimming in the afternoon? She would get the heat adjusted on the woodstove, and then she would leave that regulated as best she could. She'd take us down to the little creek behind our house and she'd teach us to swim. By the time I was old enough, I had to learn by her telling me what to do. But Mama got right in the water and taught the others. And yet, she never swam herself. But she was old by the time I learned to swim. Why, she was forty when she had me. And when I was born, I had a brother Larry, who was two, and another brother four, and a sister eight, and a sister ten. It's hard, you know, to be that old and to have all your little ones."

Dixie blew her hair off her face, her bangs flying out from her forehead, then with her long, bowed fingers pushed the remaining strands behind her ears. Her legs were crossed. The top leg swung back and forth with long, hard bounces. From the TV room, the light beamed onto the linoleum kitchen floor.

"Lots of times, Mama'd fix cookies or we'd have a picnic. But practically every afternoon in the summer, up until late August—they call that dog days—when she was canning, we'd go down and get cool at the creek. And Mama, she canned all summer long from early spring till late fall. Just like I do. Your tomatoes and apples and different things like that come on in the fall. So you can about eight months out of the year. And I remember putting kraut down. And pickles. We made fourteen-day pickles. It took fourteen days to go through all the steps. And Mama made slaw out of a great big old kraut cutter.

"And then every year in the fall, we'd take jars to the county fair. We were in 4-H Club. But my mother also took her different vegetables into the fairs. A lot of times we'd win first prize for the biggest watermelon. Ever since I was a little child I would take some of my beets. I raised those in my daddy's garden. He peddled his vegetables in town. And he also sold some at hospitals. There was a nun in the Catholic hospital over in Pittsburg, Kansas, that would come and buy maybe thirteen bushels of beets from Daddy.

"I raised beets from the seventh grade on. That was the way I earned my money. Some summers I'd earn as much as seventeen dollars. That was rich back then, enough to get a lot of my school clothes. Well, I mean I could buy enough material for all my clothes. In those days you could get thirty-five-cents-a-yard material. And I'd even have some money left over for shoes and other things like that.

"So I would take my beets to the fair. And I would also gather different varieties of things from the garden. And if they won fifty cents, or seventy-five or a dollar, you know, if they won first, second or third, it made spending money so you could ride something on the midway."

In the beginning, Dixie entered county fairs to earn pin money, but as she matured, she transformed canning from a necessity to an art, an expression of her role as, first, farm daughter, then farm wife. Over time, the arrangements and combinations of the vegetables in her jars became more and more elaborate. Color, texture, shape, all were crucial. When she canned, Dixie cared as much for beauty as for function.

"I would can green beans with two perfect rows on top of each other, all the way around. And with pickles, I would get them exactly the same size, and layer them in two rows around the pint jar. And then the beets, I would save the juice to keep the dark color. I would get all the little beets precisely the same size. And then with cooked beets, you've got to leave the stem in or they'll bleed to death and turn white. And I always strained and strained that juice to make sure there weren't any particles in it."

During a TV commercial, the boys asked Dixie for popcorn. She rummaged around in one of the lower cupboards until she found a cast-iron pan, its sides sticky with oil, then poured in the kernels, the family's home-grown, organic variety, and began shimmying the pan over the burner. As the oil heated, the corn released its aroma.

"Now with peaches, you had to be careful. I would skin them and lay them on top of each other. And I'd go clear to the top to make the jar look really neat. And then I always lined my lids up. The Ball on my lid with the Ball on my jar. Or my Kerr with my Kerr. In those days, you couldn't just go and buy new ones. You used what you had for years. So I used to work a lot, probably more than I had to. But it gave me a sense of joy, particularly to be a young farm wife and contribute in that way."

Dixie dumped the freshly popped corn into a Corning Ware bowl, then doused it with sea salt and butter from their cows. Travis headed back to the TV room with the bowl, offering it with a wave in our direction. Then he pitched his head back and dropped a few kernels onto his tongue.

"I'd take dill pickles to the fair. Sweet potatoes. String beans. Tomatoes, pears and apples. Oh, yes, and piccalilli. That was a recipe handed down from one of my grandmothers. It's a relish. It's made with green tomatoes, onions, cabbage and green and red peppers. At the end of the season, we gathered all the ingredients up. Oh, how we loved piccalilli! I used to set down with a spoon and eat a whole pint of it.

"And I made lots of jel. I won prizes for that. You'd have to strain and strain it. I would make wild plum jel. Or wild strawberry. We had a lot of different wild things growing on our land. You know, those wild strawberries are so delicious. Somebody said they should never be put in the same mouth as regular strawberries. And I think they're right."

When Dixie first married, she maintained two gardens, a small one at home and her old beet patch on her parents' acreage. At home she grew mostly lettuce, spinach, chard—cool-weather crops that bear quickly and require frequent cultivation. At her father's, where she had more room, she sowed the slower and more expansive growers like tomatoes and squash, crops that require less attention and more sun.

"I still plant two gardens. But not at once. A lot of times in the fall, when I get the summer vegetables out, I put in lettuce and radishes. Spinach does real well, too, then. And so do collards, peas, kale, turnips and parsnips. And I always plant varieties of tomatoes that come on in the fall. I like to do the bulk of my canning then. It's not so hot. And the kids are all in school. You know, I garden to put food on our table. Just like Mama."

We spent that night at Dixie's, in an old aluminum trailer she had lived in when she first became ill and was too reactive even to remain with her family. The trailer was parked two hundred feet from the house, and the rain, which let up slightly before we went to bed, pinged off the roof all night.

The next morning the sun shone. By seven o'clock, Dixie, a laundry basket propped under one arm, an egg basket dangling from the other wrist, was striding across the yard to the clothesline, where she hung out four pairs of bib overalls and four workshirts to dry. The three dogs sniffed and whined at her feet. The rain had cleared the sky of clouds and cooled the air. Ruts in the lane were filled with water, and a puddle in the middle of the yard reflected the barn at the head of the drive. Next to the barn strutted the wild turkey the Petersons had received special permission to raise, his black-and-white tail feathers fanned out with a bronzy iridescent sheen. Nearby, a larger pen housed a billy and a nanny goat, a couple of cows and Honky, the goose.

On the east side of the house, underneath an ash tree, Dixie had created a cornucopia of homegrown watermelons, gourds and squash in anticipation of our visit. The clothes hung, she ushered us toward this horn of plenty, with over a hundred fruits and vegetables cascading onto the ground—reds, oranges, greens, yellows, tans, whites, ambers—all against the deep, dewy green of the grass. At the head of the arrangement, Dixie had propped a handmade willow-reed basket piled with plump tomatoes against a fifty-pound pumpkin.

"As a child, I enjoyed the smell of the fresh-plowed soil and loved its feel under my feet. It would always be a joy on a warm, sunny day for our family to gather together and rake the garden down and set the rows. We had string and we'd mark it off just perfect. We'd make the rows with a little push plow. From the age of four or five, I was allowed to have a few short rows of what I used to call my own little garden. And after a rain in the spring, I would run out in the morning to see how much my plants had grown.

"But the gardens I remember were much earlier than our gardens nowadays. Our seasons have changed. We used to be able to plant real early. February 14, they always put in lettuce. And they planted potatoes on Saint Patrick's Day. Now we can't do that in this area or the things will freeze. But I remember when I was little, at Easter time the lettuce and onions would be up so pretty. Instead of planting the lettuce in rows, sometimes Daddy and Mama would spread it over the whole bed. And we had these tall flowers out in the garden, too.

"Once, when my mama was down working in the garden, I almost got killed. I was only three years old and our neighbor came to shoot our dog because he had eaten some sheep. I was standing there at the edge of the garden and the neighbor cocked his rifle and aimed at Trouble—that was our dog's name. The neighbor just raised up on his buckboard without saying a word. He did! He put the reins down and got up in the seat and, with one leg up, aimed the gun.

"Well, I was standing behind the dog because I was real shy when I was little. And I screamed. Then my mama turned around. She couldn't see too well because she was in the flowers where we hid our Easter baskets in the spring, and by that time the flowers were a couple feet high—all different kinds of spring flowers and a huge bed of tiger lilies. When my mama raised up, all she saw the neighbor do was pick up the reins and take out real fast. She didn't actually see the gun. But I was positive that I had. Later, my dad went to the neighbor and made him look in his own dog's mouth. And the dog had wool all over his teeth.

"Daddy wasn't a farmer. He was a carpenter. But when we kids was little, he always had huge watermelon patches. Even up to ten acres. And he always had a watermelon joke and he would tell it millions of times. It was about these guys who were going to make a bet. They told this other guy they would give him fifty dollars if he would eat a fifty-pound watermelon. And the guy said, 'Well, I'll have to be gone for a little bit, and when I come back, I'll tell you if I'll take the bet.' So, he went away and then came back pretty soon, and told his friends, 'Yeaaah. I'll make that bet with you. I know I can eat that much melon.' His friends looked at him and asked, 'How come you know you can eat a fifty-pound watermelon?' The guy said, 'I know I can eat one now because I just went home and ate one!'"

A light wind fluttered through the clothes on the line. Dixie clamped her straw hat onto her head and pushed the strap of her tank top higher on her shoulder. Her top leg bobbed up and down, her sandal flying out from her foot, then thwacking back against her heel. It was midmorning, the air heavier now, the light yellower. The sun shone through the dense needles of the pine windbreak along the north edge of the yard. In front of the house, a thick lawn sloped down to the gravel road and the wooden mailbox with its nameplate, "The Bob Petersons," nailed along the side.

"You know, now my brother Larry keeps a garden for me so I have enough to eat. But until I got sick, I always had huge gardens. And our kids always used to help, too. Just like we did when I was little. I used to send Starla and Mark—those are our two married children—every day to get onions for the table. And I remember one time they came in with their arms just packed, and they told me, 'Mama, we picked them all.' When I asked them what for, they said, 'Every day you ask us to go out and get some green onions, so we just thought we'd help you and get them all at once.' And another time, I sent Starla down to get some potatoes. And she

came back so proudly with all these little bitty ones. You know, about the size of your thumb. And I said to her, 'Well, honey, why did you get such small potatoes?' And she answered, 'I got all the little ones so they'd be easier to peel, Mom.'"

Starla, the second oldest of the Peterson brood, was a foster child, taken into the household through Barton County, Missouri, and quickly adopted as one of Dixie and Bob's own. "We had some trouble with the community when we first got Starla. Everybody said she was a Negro because of her kinky hair. But I told them that was ridiculous. She was Italian, and that explained why her hair was so curly. And you know, Bob and I just love little ones so much, we would surely have taken in more if it hadn't of been for me getting so sick. I was never afraid of work."

Sparked with nervous energy, Dixie is always in motion. And when she works, she moves with intensity and speed—peeling, slicing, chopping, grating in the kitchen, pinning out clothes, gathering eggs, filling troughs in the yard. Between chores, she whips off scarves, curtains and purses on the same Singer she used as a teenager; soaks, dries and weaves the reeds for the collection of baskets she sells; or pens designs for her line of stationery which features farm scenes and whimsical animal portraits. Even when she's relaxing, Dixie continues to move, jiggling her leg, scratching her arm, flicking back her hair.

"At first I gardened just like Daddy did. But after the herbicides came in style, Bob and I used those. Now, Daddy never used chemicals. They wasn't really well known in those days. But when I was a young farm wife, there was so much propaganda that the chemicals were good, we used them just like everybody else. As I look back, I see I used too much Sevin. Then I got sick. And our doctor became concerned because the twins were sick, too. They had diarrhea and rashes. We didn't put it all together for a while. Later, when I went to Dr. William Rhea's Environmental Illness Unit in a hospital in Dallas, Texas, nineteen chemicals was found in my bloodstream from the farm sprays in this area.

"Five years ago, we changed our garden and farm completely, using no chemicals whatsoever—no fertilizers, no herbicides, no insecticides. And it's been a challenge. But with my brother Larry's help, we've been able to grow plenty for ourselves, and had some to sell and even share with others. Now we raise our food the way they did years ago. You know, most people have a garden they put chemicals on. First they have chemically treated seeds. People don't know this, but practically all seeds will have formalde-hyde coating to keep the bugs from eating them, and to activate them when they start to grow. And then people will fertilize with chemicals, then use a herbicide to keep the weeds away and an insecticide to get rid of bugs.

"And when people buy food at the supermarket, they have no idea what they're eating. The University of Texas had a book called *Safety for Texas*. They said that commercial cabbage was usually sprayed seventeen times— if I remember right. And think about it, cabbage plants grow where their leaves are up, and so they hold that pesticide. And you know what else? Now they came out with a systemic pesticide. And I read in the catalogue: 'Use this on your tomatoes. Worms will bite the plant and die.' Well, we the American people need to wake up. If it's going to kill a bug, it's going to do damage in our bodies."

When they first started gardening without chemicals, the Petersons also stopped deep plowing. Chemicals and mechanical tilling destroy the soil's microorganisms and beneficial bacteria. They also kill the worms. "In my Daddy's garden, the soil was healthier. He tilled by hand. By deep plowing, we make it so the earth can't breathe. The first foot or so of dirt has a lot of living organisms in it. And when you turn that upside down, it puts the good, live soil on the bottom, and chokes and smothers it out. So we just stopped doing that. That's one reason our soil's healthier. And then we use organic humus. That gets the trace minerals back into your soil. Around here, for example, there's no calcium/magnesium left. There is a doctor who studies the soil, and he claims if you have trace minerals, the weeds, or at least the bad weeds, won't take over. If you look at gardens, and especially fields, where chemicals have been used, you'll see that the weeds have grown worse and worse.

"We also use our own organic fertilizers. Now, when you get into fertil-izer, you've got to be careful. A lot of people will go to a horse farm. And you know they spray horses with insecticides for your flies. That really contaminates them. And a lot of your cattle now are really laced with anti-biotics and hormones. So you've got to let their manure decompose at least two years."

Other commonly used mulches can be dangerous also, Dixie explained. Lawn-care services use chemicals to fertilize, and to kill weeds, so most grass clippings are contaminated. Hay is usually grown in chemically sprayed fields. Newspaper is laced with formaldehyde and lead during pro-

cessing and printing. Even the plastic that people put down between garden rows emits phenol when heated by the sun. But leaves make a good
mulch. And the Petersons use prairie hay. And organic hay, when they can
find it. And sawdust, not green but aged.

"My brother Larry is a carpenter, so he gets sawdust from his shop to
put out in his garden. But he only uses the hardwood shavings. Softwood
puts off turps, and Larry killed his tomatoes one year with pine shavings.
One of the farmers around here is even using sawdust as fertilizer. He got
sensitive to herbicides, so he quit using chemicals, just like we did. His
farm is right by a sawmill, and he started making piles of sawdust and
chicken manure. He composts those together, and puts that on his fields.

"And Larry's done something really funny with his strawberries. He pens
the geese in the strawberry patch and lets them eat up all the weeds. He's
got three geese in there now, and I don't think he's seen one dandelion all
summer. Of course, he has to be sure to take the geese out before the fruit
comes ripe."

The transition from chemical to organic farming is cumbersome. Crops
require daily scrutiny for insect infestations, and fields must be cultivated
constantly. "These last five years, Bob has had to work really hard to farm.
He and the boys come home so hungry. That's why I try to give my family
a big dinner every day they are out in the fields. But even if they're so tired,
it's a nice feeling to know that we are eating good food, and that it is not
having an accumulating bad effect on our health."

Dixie and her family have suffered. The financial costs of transforming
their farm into an organic operation continue to be enormous. And although her health has improved, Dixie remains isolated in her house most
of the time, unable to eat in restaurants, socialize, or attend the boys' football games because of the heavy application of herbicides to maintain the
field. The perfume in the air even keeps her from church on Sundays. And
her rare excursions to K-Mart require an oxygen mask. In wrestling with
her suffering, Dixie, who considers herself a dedicated Christian, relies on
her religion, which she says "ministers" to her in her darkest hours. She
also depends on her humor, both to lighten the atmosphere for family and
friends, and to camouflage her pain.

"Did I tell you about my twins when they were little? The doctor told us
to potty train them in a tin can. He said it would be easier than running to
the john all the time. And we had three babies to diaper and put to bed

every night. Well, one night I watched Bob use the can with the twins, stick it up on the shelf above the divan, then diaper the boys and carry them off to bed. And I thought, Boy, is that organized! Tomorrow, I'll have to try it. So the next day at naptime, I diapered Travis and let Troy and Tron go in the can. When they were finished, I put it up on the shelf just like Bob did. Then I carried the boys to bed. And I was so proud of myself. But just as I got them all to sleep, someone knocked at the door. It was the new minister and his wife—they had never met me before. I had organized people to fix up a parsonage for them and they had come to thank me. Well, they sat down, and then Travis cried, so I went and picked him out of his bitty bed and sat down on the divan. And while we were talking, Travis picked up the full can and he dumped it first over his head and then over mine. I looked at the minister and told him, 'I can explain this, really.' And he said, 'You don't need to!'"

At noon, Dixie took two butcher-wrapped packages of meat from the freezer in the kitchen, plopped a pile of potatoes on the table, then fished in one of the cupboards underneath the sink for the potato ricer. Bob and the boys would soon be coming in from the fields for the noon meal— venison steaks and burgers, riced and mashed potatoes, plus potato chips, salad, and watermelon for dessert. The boys had shot the deer themselves, and the watermelon was from Larry's garden, raised in the patch their father had tilled when they were children, a sandy hilltop on the old Hobson place, just across the road from Larry's house.

"By gardening organically we have found so many ways to stop using chemicals. We plant marigolds in our vegetables, and they keep a lot of the bugs away. So do onions and garlic. And we use Basic H by Shaklee for spray. Bugs have a protective wax-like coating, and if you take two or three tablespoons of Shaklee's with a gallon of water and spray that on your garden, the bugs will all die. We also use hot pepper, garlic and onion in a blender, along with water. That concoction gets rid of the cabbage worm.

"Another good way to deal with worms is you take nylon hose and put it over a head of cauliflower or broccoli when it's small, and the worms will never penetrate that. The hose just stretches as the plant grows. And to-matoes, they do especially well with magnesium. That's what Epsom salt is. My neighbor uses a tablespoon of Epsom salt when she plants her to-matoes. It really makes them grow."

Dixie rinsed a head of romaine lettuce. With one hand, she shook off the

water in a few quick flicks. With the other, she reached over to the stove and flipped the venison burgers, then began tearing the lettuce leaves and dropping them into the laminated wood-grain plastic bowls lined up along the counter. Next, she plunked the riced potatoes into another pan. The oil sizzled.

"I've asked lots of organic gardeners what they use for bugs, and you know what some of them answer? 'My thumb and index finger.' And Bob and I send the kids out to the garden with buckets of soapy water and tell them to pick the squash bugs off. The bugs die as soon as they hit the water. Doing it by hand that way might not be too much fun, but it's one safe way of getting rid of them. You know, a bug can damage our crops, but if a bug gets into our food, it's not going to kill us. We've been geared all wrong. There's only one percent of all the insects that's harmful. Now, when we spray that one percent, we're killing the ninety-nine percent good ones that can help prevent the bad ones. Ladybugs are real good. And so are praying mantises. And oh, yes, anybody who buys ladybugs, don't just let them loose in your garden. They'll fly off and leave. You've got to keep them for a day or two, so they'll get real hungry.

"And I remember when my daddy was gardening, we'd take a branch off a tree and swish it around to chase the blister bugs away. We also used firecrackers. You could actually drive several hundred bugs out that way because they didn't like noise. And another thing my father did was weed and hoe by hand. He had to work real hard to get those weeds out."

Bob and Dixie also rotate their crops to keep the insect population down. But unlike some organic gardeners, they don't burn their plot as a form of pest and weed control, believing that scorching destroys too many beneficial bacteria. Instead, like Dixie's father, they allow guinea hens to run among the vegetables, grazing the rows and snapping up squash bugs, bean beetles and grasshoppers.

"You know, if you don't use chemicals, you won't have just one type of weed taking over your entire garden. And anyway, sometimes there's a point when your plants are ahead of the weeds, and it doesn't hurt to let the weeds go. They can help shade the plants. Larry lets his weeds grow up around his watermelons and that protects them from the August sun. And many a good bushel of tomatoes has been got from a not completely cleaned area."

On the screened porch, Dixie slipped a steaming bowl of potatoes and a platter of ground venison onto the middle of the picnic table. Soon she was back with the salad bowls and a bag of potato chips. "Dinner's just about ready," she called to Bob and the boys as they rolled into the drive. Bob washed up in the small bathroom off the kitchen while Travis, Troy and Tron stayed in the yard and practiced for the turkey-calling contest they planned to enter in the fall. Diaphragm callers in their mouths, they imitated the cluckings, bleepings and chortlings of their wild turkey as it strutted up and down in its pen.

Dixie whizzed onto the porch with a plate of venison burgers and a bowl of mashed potatoes. She distributed paper napkins and plates, silverware from a crock, and mugs stenciled with the logo of the Oronogo football team, while with a sharp carving knife Bob cut the watermelon in half.

"I remember Daddy would take us out to his watermelon patches and we would see all those melons. And he would gently bust one open so the heart would all fall away. He would give the rest of the kids usually slices or pieces. But me and Larry, the smallest, Mom would strip us down to training pants and Daddy would give us one of those huge hearts. And I can still see it, with the seeds and water dripping down our tummies.

"When you garden, you pick vegetables according to God's own timetable. You're supposed to pick things when they're ripe. But when you buy out of the grocery store, it may have been picked three or four weeks early.

So it's not going to have the right texture. It's not going to have the right vitamin and mineral content. And another thing, seeing things grow really ministers to everybody. Children get so excited that they can put a little seed that has no life into the soil, and all of a sudden it turns to life and beautiful colors."

Travis, Troy and Tron straddled the picnic bench and Dixie pried open a Ball jar of beets, the rounds deep red, in even layers up to the neck. "I've always enjoyed hearing the *ping, ping* of the jars as they seal. And I love looking at my canning on the shelves. It's really an art. And it heals me to see my own work around because I think we've lost something important when other people do everything for us."

In his pen, the turkey crowed. The dogs took off after a kitten that had strayed from its littermates in the henhouse. A combine crunched up the road. Dixie joined hands with Bob, Travis, Tron and Troy, arms resting on the red-and-white plastic cloth, and together she and the boys waited for Bob to say grace.

# 2  Succession

I love that picture of my husband. He looks so natural. He was such a happy man. He loved to gather things out of his garden. I used to say to myself, Oh, I wish he wouldn't plant so much. But he did anyway. He even gardened an empty lot up the block. I never gardened until he was gone. Of course, I'd watched him do it, so I knew how. And if he needed help with tending, why, I'd do that. But when he died, I began gardening almost as much as he did. And I kind of surprised myself with that.

—MARY SORENSEN, *Iowa City, Iowa*

I used to get together with Roland Stone. Did you know he died this spring? And he was young, too. He was a professor over at Knox College. And he lived three houses away from us. He had the idea of raising a lot of Chinese vegetables. He used to come down and talk some. What I always noticed about him was that he tried to be my equal. Not like other people at the college. If you've ever read anything in sociology magazines, you know custodians or janitors like me always used to live in the basements of buildings where it was dark and dirty.

But Roland always treated me real nice. We talked about gardening. I remember one time he came down with his hat and long coat. We were shoveling manure out of a pickup. And here he is, picture perfect, next to this old truck of manure. I think that's how we started talking about gardening. He told me that he and his wife, Nancy, had a garden in Thailand and liked to grow Chinese vegetables. So we got together and made a list and sent away for the seeds. Then Roland died. But Nancy and I decided we would raise his garden anyway.—RICK LIPSKY, *Galesburg, Illinois*

Now that you've seen all my vegetables, I want to show you something else. Right here, in front of my house, I have seventeen geranium plants. When my mother was still living, she'd come every spring for Easter. She'd have geraniums she'd have started in the house, and she'd give them to me. And she'd say, "Now you put them right here, so I can see them when I come." So I kind of got a thing going. For every year my mother's been gone, I plant a geranium.—HAROLD BECKMAN, *Bricelyn, Minnesota*

# Succession

## An Interview with Bill Hatke

*I was born and spent the first eighteen years of my life in Keu-*
*terville, Idaho. After attending college at Loyola University in*
*Chicago, where I received an undergraduate degree in philoso-*
*phy, and the University of Kansas, where I received a Ph.D. in*
*sociology, I decided to leave the world of academia and return*
*to my first love, gardening, to make a living. I have lived hap-*
*pily ever after.*

—Bill Hatke, Lawrence, Kansas

"**L**AWRENCE MAN GETS BY ON ONLY $120 A YEAR," Bill Hatke read the headline, then the lead paragraph from the *Kansas City Times* feature on him. "I have no electricity, phone, running water, TV, stereo, or other money-gobbling habits. And I'm the happiest guy in the world for it."

Photographs of Bill accompanied the article: one of Bill's smoke-stained Ph.D. diploma nailed to the wall above the wood-burning stove he uses for cooking meals and heating his four-room house; another of the bearded Bill reading by the light of an oil lamp, with his thicket of curls bent close to the page; and a third of Bill, lean and muscular, in one of his seven gardens. Here, he is barefoot and bare-chested, his head thrown back as he pours water from an old jug into his mouth.

"You know, of all the things I told that reporter, I thought what she published was rather odd. See, she interviewed me for two days, and we talked about almost every God-awful thing you can possibly imagine. I mean, the whole focus of her article was, 'He has no utilities. He doesn't even have a car.' Now, I ask you, why would she focus on that, when we talked about so many other subjects? We talked about Zen Buddhism. We talked about the dropouts of the sixties. And, my God, we talked about gardening. We talked about sweet corn and squash bugs. And I told her all about my methods for storage. But none of that appears."

For Bill, any listener is an opportunity to perform. Like an actor in the commedia dell'arte, he struts, he swaggers, he sways, he giggles, flashing his white teeth, his voice high-pitched and singsong one minute, deep and resonant the next. His costume: a washed-out football jersey and castaway chinos, crudely cut off at the knees and splotched with an accretion of food and gardening stains, the crotch loosely patched with childlike stitches in black thread. The setting: Bill's front yard, a jumble of vegetables—okra fanning out over the steps to his house, green beans winding around the fence and gate, zucchini sprawling up and over the curb and, here and there, patches of beets and carrots poking through open spaces between the vines.

"I mean, the woman from the *Kansas City Times* never even explained why I started to garden. I'm a University of Kansas dropout. I have my Ph.D. in sociology. Well, I guess the article says that. But I decided I didn't want to work in my field—criminology. There were plenty of jobs, but it was basically working with the leftovers of society. And this society has a

*Bill Hatke*

way of creating so many leftovers and so much waste in terms of human beings. I didn't want to be part of that, and I decided to find another way to live.

"I always knew how to garden, and for me it was a catharsis. When I was finishing my courses at the university, I was pretty involved with the intellectual stuff. Gardening was a way to get away from that—to get back to something that was purely physical, something that would respond. I guess I needed some kind of therapy, so I started growing things and I liked it so much, I thought, Why don't you just do this for a living?"

Bill's hands swooped through the air, gliding, soaring, then dropping until they settled on his dense beard, the fingertips massaging his jaw and chin. At his feet, a cabbage butterfly flitted among the cucumber vines. On his ankle, where he had scratched a chigger bite, a trickle of blood thickened and turned dark.

"I learned to garden when I was six years old in northern Idaho. My mother pretty well supported a family of eight kids on what she grew. Dad produced the beef cattle and the deer and the hogs. But my mother did all the vegetables and fruits. And then when I was thirteen, I worked for some years in a convent garden with Benedictine nuns. It was Saint Gertrude's

Convent and Academy in Cottonwood, Idaho. They had a huge garden and it was a private school. They charged, well, at that time it was only $125 a semester. What I did was, I earned that and my book money by working in the garden.

"Of course, the convent garden was different from my mother's. The school was out on a prairie, so the sisters could grow many crops my mother couldn't—for example, corn and pumpkins, cantaloupe, cucumbers and beans. Where I grew up, we were higher in the mountain valley. My mother raised all the cold-weather crops: peas, lettuce, spinach, turnips, cabbage, rhubarb, beets. Oh, yes, and Irish potatoes.

"And then we had strawberries. The strawberry patch was on the south slope of a high hill. The draws would freeze—you know, those areas between the higher hills—so we planted strawberries and things like that up high. The draws around us were formed by runoff that eventually found its way to the Salmon River. The Snake River Gorge was about ten miles from the house."

Bill grew up in the wilderness, the old family homestead surrounded by a dense forest of pine, and white and red fir trees. On one side of the Hatkes', there were no neighbors. On the other side, the closest family lived two miles through the timber. The nearest town, Keuterville, Idaho, with a population of twenty-two, was ten miles away. Carved out of the forest, the town consisted of one street, known by the locals as the Keuterville-Cottonwood road. Today Keuterville's population has swelled to thirty-five, and the old post office and the Keuterville Tavern/Store are still functioning. The town even boasts its own highway district headquarters.

And Keuterville still has lots of spunk. Three years ago it celebrated its centennial. Displays of quilts and saws, including several tree climbers, and an old steam engine that one of the residents hauled out of his garage, lined the road during the day. At night, after everyone had gorged themselves on hot dogs and Coke, with the smell of pine heavy in the air, young and old danced in the streets to the music of a band imported from Cottonwood, where sometime after Bill's graduation Saint Gertrude's had metamorphosed into Prairie High School. Bill's brother Hank, who lives in a new house he built on the old family property, urged Bill to attend the celebration.

"But I wouldn't go, even if I had the money. Keuterville represents a way of life I'm not very fond of. My mother had a nervous breakdown, and because of the rural way of life so many people romanticize these days, the community just ignored her. And believe me, everybody knew my mother. My grandfather was one of the founders of Keuterville. And my father was born in the same house that my mother had her children in. Of course, the fact that my grandfather founded the town didn't mean my family prospered. We were very poor. When I got to college, I figured out that my parents raised eight kids on twelve hundred dollars a year.

"In fact, we were so poor that just about everything we ate came out of the garden or off the land. Oh, we would never buy anything but sugar or coffee. Mom made her lard and she made her soap until I was about thirteen. Then civilization arrived. Everything came later to us because of how backwoods we were. I must have been nine or ten before we got electricity. I remember sitting around the living room table with a coal lamp. And we had no tractors. We did have an old beat-up truck. That was the only mechanical thing. Everything else was moved with horses.

"We had a horse-drawn mower and wagons to bring the hay into the barn. And we manured out the barn every year by hand, too. You know, we hauled the manure down to the garden in the spring, or maybe in the fall. See, the barn just had a dirt floor, and in the wintertime, we let the horses and cattle in out of the storms. When we got to the manuring depended on how the work load was going. Manuring out the barn was something you did after you cut up all the hay, or once you had all the cattle moved and branded."

For a while after leaving home, Bill lived a cosmopolitan life, attending Loyola University of Chicago, then pursuing a degree in criminology at the University of Kansas. At one time he even owned a condominium, which he later sold to buy his four-room house in a residential neighborhood in East Lawrence, Kansas. Then he dropped out and, whether by design or happenstance, evolved a life which replicates his childhood in Idaho. He quit his two jobs, one analyzing social science surveys on computer, the other stacking paper at a printing firm, and began gardening, progressively paring down his lifestyle in order to become self-sufficient. First he eliminated the phone, then the gas. Next the pipes burst, and he never repaired the plumbing. Electricity was the last amenity Bill gave up—he knew he would miss his radio.

Now, a cistern which collects rainwater for drinking has replaced the bathtub and toilet in Bill's bathroom. In the kitchen, shelves of dusty glass canning jars take up the space where the range used to sit. And until the city made him tear them down, Bill had a greenhouse jutting out of one side of his kitchen and a chicken coop incorporated into his living room.

Self-sufficiency is not Bill's only goal. Ever since he began gardening, he has been determined not to become greedy, rarely allowing himself to be seduced by the trappings of civilization. "If I have too much money, I start wanting things." To limit his income, Bill has let certain vegetable plots lie fallow, and last summer he curtailed his gardening work to four hours per day. By reining himself in and selling his produce selectively to the Lawrence Food Co-op as well as several local restaurants, he earns just the money he needs—enough to pay his ninety-eight dollars in yearly property taxes, plus incidental expenses like instant coffee and one movie a year. What he can't pay for he barters: he babysits in exchange for use of a washing machine; he helps a stonemason in order to borrow the mason's truck for hauling; and he supplies zucchini to the friend who recharges his radio batteries.

Despite his modest needs, Bill gardens prolifically. He also gardens simply, his methods identical to those his mother taught him when he was six. "I don't plow my garden and I don't till. I work the ground by hand. People say, 'What do you mean, you work the garden by hand? Do you really go out there and get on your hands and knees?' No, I use a hoe and a rake and a shovel, for crying out loud! I just don't use any motorized mechanisms. But not at all because I romanticize rural life. Only because my goal is to save money. That's why I don't fertilize, and that's why I don't irrigate, either. That's something else that costs. If it dies, it dies. For the same reason, I don't use insecticides. I support myself off my garden. That's the only income I have.

"And I'm lucky because people have always given me space. My first garden was a small plot sandwiched in between concrete slabs in downtown Lawrence. And that pattern of friends offering me plots continues. I could be talking to somebody at their house, and there might be a patch of unused land, and they would let me plant it. At one time, I was gardening about twelve or fourteen plots all over town. I counted up the other day, and since I've been here, I've gardened fifty-six different places. I ride all over on my bike, and carry my tools and harvest in a little cart attached to the rear wheels.

"I haul my wood around in my little cart, too. You see, I can get all the wood I need for my stove just riding around town. In fact, when the city came the last time, they had me get rid of some of my lumber. My pile was excessive, they said. There's some kind of code that states you can store a two-year supply, but you can't store more. Oh, yes, it's code time again. How I love those little codes!"

Once again aware of his audience, Bill impersonated the housing inspector, wagging his finger, his voice rising into falsetto as he giggled and pranced around the okra on his bare, slender toes. Then his face grew severe, his voice ministerial. "Of course, being in the middle of town, trouble with the city is unavoidable. You know, especially when you have neighbors to the south who complain. Mine have two or three domestic arguments a day, and I have to listen to them screaming about *me*. 'There used to be a nice lawn over there. Now look what he's done to it. I can't stand it anymore. I have allergies. I just can't stand it.' But I want you to know something. The way I grow things *does* make sense."

Bill's backyard is where he makes sense of gardening, and the yard is a microcosm of his life. It expresses all the passion, skills, ingenuity and expertise he has acquired since he worked with his mother on the family homestead, deep in the woods at the base of the arm where Idaho reaches up toward British Columbia, and the Nez Percé used to roam. In the 50 × 100-foot lot behind his house, Bill has created a one-man agricultural economy—planting, cultivating, harvesting and storing the nourishment he needs to survive, as well as recycling his own wastes. There are beehives by the back door and piles of corn drying on the ground, the husks splitting open. There are beans, okra, peppers, butternut squash, tomatoes, asparagus and strawberries growing in cages, on poles, in patches, in mounds. There are ladders leaning up against pear and apple trees, and shovels, spades and hoes resting on the ground. There are a cache pit (a hole dug into the ground for storing vegetables), a woodpile and a composting toilet, all bounded by a back fence patched from old boards, pieces of cardboard, carpeting and corrugated metal.

"You can see this garden doesn't follow any recognizable plan. I plant as space comes open. First, I planted everything in carrots and beets on one side. And on the other side, I had leeks and onions and garlic. And of course, there are strawberry beds running through. What's happened then is these crops give out, and then I plant the later stuff. I put in peppers and eggplant with the carrots and beans. Then I put watermelon where the leeks and onions were. I also scattered okra helter-skelter. Then, if I see another spot open, I put something else in. What I put in depends on the time of the year, but I never plant in rows. Some people will go to the seed catalogue in February and start designing their little gardens. I never lay out a plan. I garden more like this: Well, now it's the beginning of March and I need to get all my peas planted.

"But this kind of gardening really works. Look over there at those butternut squash. There are fifteen of them all from one hill. Most people don't get any squash because of the bugs. I've tried to deal with them manually in years past. What I do now is plant my squash early. Then I have something planted right next to it. Like this year it was peppers. Peppers do real well growing in the shade of the squash. When the squash dies, the peppers take over the area."

Bill follows the same method with lettuce and spinach. Once these cool-weather crops begin to die back, he plants cantaloupe and watermelon among the drying plants, allowing the melons to rush out and cover the ground in late spring. Then, at the end of the summer, triggered by the cooler temperature of the earth, the lettuce and spinach seeds from the first planting sprout. "It's got to get pretty cold, actually. When the soil reaches 50 degrees, the cantaloupe and watermelon die and the other plants are free to grow. And I cultivate peas that way, too.

"I guess I've invented this method, although all I did was notice it happening. Once I planted peas, then watermelon over them. In the fall, I noticed that the peas grew right up through the melon vines. Now, the books tell you to plant peas in the middle of August, but my peas start growing about mid-July. Oh, and this is very important, you just let the pea patch die down, and then they plant themselves. So for peas, lettuce and spinach, you basically weed the area by planting melons."

Most of Bill's gardening revolves around this succession method of planting. He sows black-eyed peas or beans and strawberries together, the legumes shading the berries and protecting them from heat and drought. He also plants sweet corn and cherry tomatoes in the same area, reaping an early harvest of corn by mid-July, as the tomatoes continue to climb up the stalks. The sweet corn keeps the sun from hitting the tomatoes directly and protects them from scorch. And Bill pairs sweet potatoes and turnips, leaving one turnip from his spring garden to go to seed, then in June planting sweet potatoes where the turnips once flourished. Later, when the frost kills the sweet potato crop, the turnips begin maturing all over again.

"You know, I really like thinking about these succession plantings because I've been working with them for so long now. All I have to do is think about the different gardens I've had and what worked well together, and I could talk about it forever. Of course, when I'm talking succession, I'm talking early crop, late crop. I say to myself, What am I going to plant here in the spring that will be taken over in the summer and will come back again in the fall?"

There are some vegetables, Bill warns, that do not work well together. Onions and leeks have a tendency to stunt beans. And peanuts do poorly with anything, like okra, that grows above them, or like watermelon or cantaloupe, that vines around them. Peanuts need room to spread as they grow. And Bill has discovered that planting corn and beans together is counterproductive. The corn ends up blocking too much of the sun, and the beans do not produce very well. "Unless, of course, you do what the oldtimers did. Do corn, four to a hill, maybe four feet between hills. Then, around the corn, put Kentucky Wonder pole beans, the beans being planted, oh, approximately four weeks after the corn. Then the corn will mature and the beans will wrap themselves around the stalks, using them as poles. The trick to this combination is all in the coordinating. If you plant the beans too early, they drag the corn down. And if you plant them too late, they can't sprout before the corn begins to shade them."

Bill's planting techniques are genial, the inventions of imagination and a finely honed faculty for observation. But more than anything else, these methods are sparked by a paradoxical combination of choice and necessity—by Bill's quest to live outside of convention, yet at the same time to sustain himself with the income of garden plots borrowed from friends and acquaintances all around Lawrence.

The same impetus led Bill to begin saving his seeds. "Why spend money for something you can get for free?" To harvest seeds, Bill simply lets many of his vegetables grow for a full year, leaving everything in the ground during the winter, mulched with hay at least a foot deep to keep the plants from freezing. As with most of Bill's gardening, the key to this method is timing. He spreads the mulch only at the very end of the season, after a good freeze, and removes it as soon as the ground begins to warm in the spring so the plants can begin growing again and eventually produce their seed pods. Beets and carrots were the first plants Bill insulated in this manner, the carrots surprising him by sending up exquisite lacelike clusters of miniature white flowers.

"Of course, with carrots, the real trick is just to get there at the right moment. They shoot up and start maturing, and there's about a week period when the seeds will stay in the pod. And if you don't get them immediately, they'll just blow away. Actually, what I do is, just as the carrot's about to mature, I pull it out and bring it inside the house and set it on newspaper. Then I shake it and the seeds come out. Sometimes I've screwed up. I've been busy, and two days after the carrots are ready, we get this big downpour, and *pshhhhhtt*, there they are in the ground already. Of course, you can just let this turn into a carrot patch the next year."

Like carrots, onions, leeks and garlic also send up seed pods which Bill sets on paper in his house. He collects tomato seeds the same way. "If you don't want it to take too long, you should squish the tomatoes so the juice runs out and the seeds can dry faster. With peppers, let them get real red, then strip the membrane off. At the bottom, you'll have a little ball of seeds. Let that dry, and when you rub it, the seeds will pop off."

Bill also recycles his sweet potatoes. But unlike most gardeners he doesn't cut up last year's crop for starts. Instead, he takes his smallest potatoes and plants entire tubers, digging down nine inches and covering them with three inches of dirt. He leaves at least one foot between plants and five feet between rows. With this method, Bill reaps twelve to fourteen huge potatoes from each plant.

"I learned about this from an old black man who used to live right across the street. He also told me to go out about a foot and a half from the hill and whack everything off the last week in August or the first week in September. That way all the energy goes back into the plant, and not the leaves. I do this in my garden and people ask, 'What in the world are you doing?' Well, I can tell you, you get gigantic potatoes that way. I get some that can make a meal for at least five people. I can also tell you it's convenient when you go to harvest. You don't have to go digging around a large area searching for the potatoes. They're all right there."

The lay and scale of Bill's backyard are too small and cluttered for sweet potatoes, which he cultivates a mile south of his house in a lot behind the backyard of the novelist William S. Burroughs, where the half-acre plot creates a radically different backdrop for Bill's expertise and sensibilities. Serene and verdant even at high noon, this garden is laid out in rows and clearly defined patches, okra on the two long sides, beans, sweet potatoes, peas, strawberries in the center. A stand of raspberries and blackberries, their brambles thick and tangled, runs along the western border.

The earth here is rich and black, the result of Bill's no-till, constant-weed method. For the five years he has gardened this plot, Bill has kept it weed free. And because he works only with hand tools, he has not disturbed the weed seeds, which often lie deep and can remain alive for as long as forty years. Bill also protects the soil in this plot by leaving most of the plants to die in place. Throughout the winter, okra, tomato and sweet potato stalks and foliage blanket the earth, breaking the rain as it beats down and keeping the soil from compacting. For additional protection, Bill might add a small layer of mulch—some leftover straw from the sale barn, but mostly lawn clippings. He also discovered that if he plants garlic throughout the rows in the spring, the sprouting bulbs help soften the ground for the next season. "And of course, I leave some of my root vegetables in over the winter. That helps the soil, too."

Bill has named the Burroughs plot his "Berry-Garlic Garden," and in it he practices what he calls his berry philosophy. He never irrigates and he never prunes. Instead, he allows foliage, either from the plant itself or from neighboring plants, to help conserve moisture. "See how green those strawberries are growing under the black-eyed peas? And we're in the middle of a drought! And then let me show you my raspberries and blackberries. With those I never cut the canes. I just let them mass and get real thick. That way they keep enough moisture in the ground to continue growing, even when there's no rain. Of course, with the blackberries, I'll whack them back so I can get a path through. But I won't prune them. You can't treat strawberries the same way, though. You need to let those move. The strawberry plant will send down a root that has a tendency to wooden and die. So, at least every two years I wipe out one whole section of strawberries and let another section grow."

Bill bent over and yanked out a tuft of lamb's-quarters, which he stuck under his left arm. Then he bent again, this time over a clump of crab grass. And again, over wild oats, each time poking the weeds under his left arm and plucking with his right hand, the fingers soon caked with dirt. "I'm sorry. I shouldn't be doing this with you here. But I can't help myself." Then he bent again, straightening seconds later, another clump of crab grass dangling from his hand. "This is my cleanest garden. Actually, all of my gardens are unique. I try to concentrate on growing different things in each one. You should see my corn-melon garden. That's really a sight!"

To reach this third garden, which is on the far north side of town, we followed Bill as he rode his bike, his implements clattering in the cart behind him, first down oak- and elm-shaded residential streets, then through Lawrence's red-brick, Tudor-style downtown, past the Eldridge Hotel, originally built in 1854 as a Free State hotel, and the old Bowersock Opera House, past the Round Corner Drug and the Paradise Cafe. As Bill pedaled, the limestone buildings of the University of Kansas rose on his left, at the summit of Mount Oread, overlooking the Kansas River valley to the north and the Wakarusa valley to the south. North of the courthouse and shopping area, and beyond Massachusetts Street, Bill reached the industrial section of town, then crossed the Kansas River and the railroad tracks, where once again he navigated residential streets, these more spread out and less solidly middle-class than those closer to the downtown and the university. On one house, the front porch was caving in. Strips of siding hung loose on another. A junked car hulked in the driveway of a third.

"This area is what they call the sandy bottom. It's the kind of soil water-

melon does so well in. According to the theory, the glacier came to the river's edge and then stopped. Everything on this side of the river is glacier deposits. They say you can go down seventeen feet and have nothing but good, fertile soil. Over on the other side of town where I live, you quickly run into clay."

A large field abutting a tiny frame house, this third garden is situated on the open Kansas prairie. Here every contour of the earth, every knoll, rise, flat and hollow seemed magnified. The sky, filled with deflated cumulus clouds, paralleled the land, dropping to meet it at the horizon line—houses and barns, trees, even blades of grass standing out sharply against the air. As if to intensify this vista, a swath of corn rose seven feet in a diagonal across the middle of the garden, while zucchini and patty pan, butternut, acorn and summer squash, cantaloupe and watermelon vines crept over the remaining surface area, their tendrils curling toward the corners of the lot. The tassels of the corn were splayed and swollen in the August heat. Under their broad, scalloped leaves, the reticulated skins of the cantaloupes turned golden, the fruit emitting a faint sticky-sweet perfume.

"All of my gardens have evolved on their own. In my Burroughs garden, along with berries and garlic I grow okra, black-eyed peas and beans, because none of those really requires rich soil. And here because of the sandy bottom, I have all my melons. And see how all that corn's growing in a band? Well, my friend the stonemason and I actually got his big dump truck stuck in the garden last year. We went to the horse farm and got a load of manure, and I told him, 'Keith, don't drive the truck down the middle there. It's really soft ground.' But he didn't listen, and we ended up shoving boards under the wheels to get them out. But once he got his truck loose, he dumped the manure just like I wanted him to. He opened up the bed, and as he drove through the garden, the manure spread itself. It was like a vision—a dump truck spreading a whole load of manure across *my* garden.

"And this year, I decided because the ground is so rich here, I'd do the heavy eaters, potatoes first, corn second, and maybe beets in the fall. And it seems to be working. Look how well the corn's doing. And there's something else I'm trying with the corn this year. I'm not popping all the suckers like I used to.

"When I worked at the convent, the nuns taught me to remove all the suckers from the stalks in order to direct energy back into the main ears.

But last year, some guy stopped by this garden one day and said, 'You know, you're wasting your time. According to the county agent, you don't have to remove the suckers anymore.' Well, I didn't believe the guy, but I told him, 'OK. I'll do a little experiment with you. Here are ten rows of corn. I'll pop the suckers off five rows and leave the suckers on the rest. But I don't believe your cock-and-bull story.' Well, it turned out the ears with the suckers were just as big as those without, and they even had an advantage. We get these incredible winds in Kansas. You pull the suckers off, and *phewww*, down go the stalks. You keep the suckers on and the corn stays up. Also, the suckers keep the weeds down. They're like a natural mulch."

Bill ducked behind a row of corn, then stuck his head out from between two stalks, and hammed a series of profiles—nose up, nose down, smiling, frowning, reflecting, winking—while he waited for us to take photographs. "You know, the cameraman from the *Times* spent eight hours taking pictures of me, but they only published three. Now don't you think that was a waste of time?" Then, with a rustle, Bill slipped down another row, popping out a few seconds later at the edge of the corn.

"You know, this garden is almost too prolific. And I don't want to have too many vegetables to sell. I want to live simply. Though not the way my parents did. People are always interpreting my life like that. But I tell them, if they think the country is such a great place to live, they should try it. Do you realize that in 1790, 90 percent of the population lived in rural areas, while in 1970, 90 percent lived in urban areas? And you have to assume that this was not just a matter of economic opportunity. It must also have been a question of individual taste. The rural environment is just not a very pleasant place to be. Here in Lawrence people are more tolerant, there's more individual freedom, there's more diversity, and in a strange way, there's a lot less hypocrisy.

"Oh, the rural area can have the veneer of a tight-knit community. But when my mother had her nervous breakdown, she was basically all alone. And we knew everyone within a distance of seventy miles. And we knew everything about them. We knew who shot whose cow, who was cross-branding, and who was blotch-branding. Those were the big scandals. And then, of course, there was moonlighting. I mean, there was nothing everybody didn't know. But they all completely ignored my mother.

"In all, she had four nervous breakdowns. Who wouldn't, with eight kids to raise. The final breakdown occurred my junior year in high school. By that time, my dad had died. I was already away at school, and the kids at home fled the situation. My mother went from 145 to 85 pounds. She couldn't even get out of bed. And the neighbors knew all about it. When I got home, I discovered her like that, and I had to take her to a state mental hospital and commit her."

Overhead, a sparrow hawk circled the corn. In the full afternoon sun, Bill's face was reddish brown, the long hairs of his eyebrows bleached, his hair peppered, the curls bushy at the temples but receding back from his forehead. His beard straggled down his cheeks and neck past his Adam's apple.

"I guess you can understand how I have a jaundiced view of the rural area. There was this creed that you care about your neighbor, but then there was also a conflicting rule or complementary ethic that said, 'Mind your own business. Don't deal with other people's dirty laundry.' Well, that ethic forced me to grow up rather quickly. You might say I never even had a childhood. But here's something to note. Yes, I think that this is very important. Gardening, even back then, never did seem to disappoint me."

Bill squatted down and began gathering melons, tapping the tiny curl at the stem end to see if it was dry and the fruit ripe. Toes disappearing into the sandy loam, he waddled from vine to vine, head down, back curved, leaning toward, then away from the earth, his skin taut across his forearms. When he rose, he had a load of green-and-white-striped watermelons and rough, ribbed cantaloupe nestled in the crook of each arm.

The harvest from Bill's seven gardens is abundant. Every summer and fall he reaps far more apples, peas, berries, beans, corn, melons, potatoes, turnips, tomatoes and squash than he needs to keep himself alive. But the gardens do more than sustain Bill physically. They give him the space and variety essential for him to play out the multiple scripts in his life. Buffoon, philosopher, Zen Buddhist, skeptic, intellectual, farmer, artist, engineer, recluse, Bill has at least as many sides as he does gardens, and he moves among them nimbly, creating a dazzling one-person performance in which life and art fully coincide.

# I Just Dug All the Harder

## An Interview with Marti Roynon

*I grew up in Rochester, Indiana, where I enjoyed, but did not*

*help with, my father's vegetable garden and my mother's flower*

*beds. I have written commercially since 1939: radio, drama,*

*educational films, television advertising, articles on food, skiing,*

*and travel. I was one of the founders of the Old Town Triangle*

*Garden Club, where we had a hundred plots on a vacant lot. By*

*gardening in the middle of Chicago, I learned to cope with dogs,*

*bugs, vandalism, and theft, and still raise beautiful strawberries.*

—Marti Roynon, Chicago, Illinois

"This shows the way the Old Town Triangle Garden Club plot looked in the very beginning. Just a dump." Marti Roynon held a photographic slide up to the light, squinting into the sun as she perched atop a barrel on a Chicago sidewalk in front of a construction site. In the slide, waist-high weeds, pushing through piles of rocks and slabs of concrete, cover an empty lot bordered by brownstones. Ailanthus saplings shoot up near the curb where parked cars form a ring around the plot. Old paint buckets, cans, fast-food cartons and beer bottles are snagged on clumps of broken paving bricks.

"The developer had torn down everything on this block to build a high-rise, but the neighborhood organized and had the area rezoned, downzoned actually, so you couldn't put up such a huge building. After that, the land went through several ownerships, each trying to buy out city hall. The last owner got the lot rezoned back again for a high-rise, and the neighborhood association fought and fought for several years. We finally lost. But in the interim, the land was a dangerous nuisance. When things became desperate, the owner put up fences, but those blew down. At last the neighborhood had a meeting with the owner and said, 'Why don't you open the lot up for gardening? Something would be happening there, at least.' So he did. The land became a gardening plot, and fifty of us cultivated the ground for nine straight years."

Marti brushed her bangs out of her eyes, an antique bracelet of carved wooden buttons dangling around her wrist. Then she slipped the slide back into its plastic box. The morning sun illuminated her henna red hair. In her youth, she could have been a silent screen star—small-boned, her cheeks high and rouged, loose curls framing her face. And Marti has made movies, not as an actress, but as a writer and advertising executive. Earlier in her career she wrote radio commercials and soap operas, and when television came into existence, she designed some of the first TV ads, including one for Stopette deodorant on "What's My Line?" and another for Viv lipstick featuring Arthur Godfrey complimenting a woman on her lips.

"I'd never even pulled a weed before I got this garden." Marti shouted over the traffic and the noise of construction which stretched from Wells to Clark streets, an entire city block. The skeleton of a high-rise building towered out of the dirt before her, the steel beams supporting workers with welding masks flipped down over their faces. A crane pivoted and hoisted

*Marti Roynon*

another beam into the air. Next to a stack of plywood, a forklift crouched, frozen in position, forks readied, two arms open to receive a load. Blue plastic tarps thrown over the top of the boards crinkled and flapped in the breeze.

"Oh, my father had a big garden when I was growing up in Rochester, Indiana. But I didn't do anything in the way of work when I was a child except make my bed and keep my room neat. We had what was called a hired girl in our house. So I didn't even pick any of my father's vegetables. And my mother had just loads of flowers. But she had help in the spring getting those beds ready. Oh, I guess I used to work with her sometimes. I'd go around carrying a basket of bulbs. My mother would say, 'Hand me a bulb.' I would hand her one, and she would put it in. This was when I was quite small. And one year when I was little, I had a pansy bed under a lilac tree, but the pansies didn't grow very well, and that was the end of my gardening experience."

Marti fished another slide out of the plastic case balanced on her knees. "Here's a shot of my first garden the summer the project began. Two men who owned a lamp shop right across the street from the lot organized the plots. They had gone over and measured out the area and put little stakes in the ground. The plots had numbers on them and everyone was assigned number such and such." Marti passed us the second slide, a garden plot staked out in the middle of the weeds and rubble.

In the transparency, the 10 × 20-foot area is divided in half. On the right side, the rows are straight and mulched with newspaper. The plants on the left are arranged in a more free-form configuration, separated by pathways of hard, brown clay. Paving bricks edge the garden, and inside their border, orange and yellow marigolds surround Swiss chard, spinach, eggplant, broccoli, lettuce, basil and oregano—all struggling their way to maturity. In the background, tomato vines secured to stakes wind up shoulder high, and in the foreground, a dented beer can caps a metal pole, twirling in the wind.

"When I first began gardening, I gardened just the way I used to ski. For over twenty years, my husband Jack and I were avid skiers. We even made several trips a year to Aspen, Colorado. And when our son, Rob, was growing up, he came along, too. Then Jack died of cancer in 1974, and shortly after that, Rob was murdered by a burglar in his apartment in Los Angeles. It was a horrible shock, but even after my family was gone, I decided to keep on skiing. I thought, There's no point in my stopping. They would be ashamed of me if I did."

During her first winter of grief, Marti skied Aspen, but more out of a sense of desperation than fun. Head down, she would push off at the top of Spar Gulch, stopping only when she reached the bottom. Friends would hail her along the way, but she streaked right by without even noticing. After a while, though, she slowed down. She began hunting for people to ski with, joined the Seventy-Plus Ski Club, and even freelanced articles about the group. "I realized that I was just skiing. I wasn't fraternizing or enjoying myself. So I made up my mind I wouldn't ski alone anymore."

In 1974 when she first began gardening, Marti found herself driven once again, concentrating on the physical act and ignoring the social context. "In my first gardens, I broke sod and prepared the whole bed by hand. I just dug and dug and dug. I needed something to work out my energies and misery. And digging is a good way to get stress out of your system."

Marti propped herself up on the barrel, arms straight, hands gripping either side. Her feet, in brown Chinese slippers, barely touched the sidewalk. Wispy curls fluttered around her face and set off her brows—thin, arched and penciled—her brown eyes and delicate nose. She patted her hand to the V-neck of her brown terry cloth dress that revealed the pale, wrinkled skin of her chest and cleavage. Another slit in her dress ran from her hem to thigh.

"Of course, everybody had to work hard those first few years. The ground had never been cultivated before. A man named Crilly had owned the original property in the Old Town Triangle. It was a small neighborhood first settled by Germans in the 1800s. Crilly built apartments called the Georgian Court on the Clark Street side. A *Turnverein*—that's a German gymnasium—ran along the Wells Street side. And the German influence remained so strong that even when I moved into the neighborhood in the 1950s, the Catholic and Protestant churches still had their sermons in German."

But before Marti and her husband ever moved into the neighborhood, the S and A Film Company had bought the *Turnverein*, and Crilly Court oldtimers reminisced about the Keystone Kops running through the streets. Gloria Swanson and Francis X. Bushman even worked out of the studio until S and A moved away. The building changed hands several more times before it was abandoned for a number of years in the 1960s, when Arthur J. Rubloff bought it to tear down and construct a high-rise.

"That's when the neighborhood association formed and the lot eventually became a garden. Originally, we had the land and a toolshed which blew over in the first high wind. But that's what we started with—the shed and the tools that we bought with our fee. We each paid three dollars and there were a hundred of us in the beginning. That three hundred dollars bought the shed and a few tools, not nearly enough to go around. You were always standing in line for a hoe."

The money also bought two hoses. One was fastened to a fire hydrant on Clark Street, with a club member assigned to attach it each evening at five o'clock. When the person didn't show up on time, a long line of irritated fellow gardeners waited by the curb. But lack of water and tools were givens. The unexpected problems were the most troublesome.

"That first year, we asked our alderman for a load of sludge, and the city spread sewage all over the lot. That was horrible stuff! Clay, sticky, and full of cadmium. I remember digging through that sludge in my first garden. Well, really, that was my second plot. When I went to get my first plot, it was buried under a heap of rubbish. So, I went back to the two young men and said, 'Look, I can't garden in this pile of concrete!' And they gave me a

plot to share with an elderly couple who thought their garden too big. I said, 'Fine, because I'm alone and I've never done any gardening.'"

The elderly couple mulched their rows with newspaper and decorated their borders with rocks and bricks they had dug up when readying the soil for planting. "If you look at this slide closely, you can see that couple's paper mulch between the rows. It was a good idea, but I didn't follow their direction because I thought it looked messy. And that first year the earth was just hardpan. I planted very little from seed, and the few things I did plant didn't do very well because the soil was so poor. When things did come up, they were immediately eaten by bugs. The garden was so full of bugs, I got nothing at the end of the season but tomatoes. But I was so proud of them, I thought my heart would burst. Of course, when you dug the ground around them, you dug up bricks and old light bulbs, rusty iron hinges and door knobs. It was just dreadful!"

Soon the elderly couple got tired of working their soil and turned over their half of the garden to Marti. For several years she worked to build up the ground in that plot, adding manure and fertilizer. Then when a space opened near the sidewalk and fire hydrant, Marti relocated. Even though the soil wasn't as enriched, her new garden was easier to irrigate. But this luxury didn't make Marti lazy. Throughout her nine years of gardening three different plots, she turned over every clump of dirt by hand.

"We had no really good shovels. I remember the best shovel I could get I borrowed from my friend Chuck. It wasn't actually a garden shovel. And it wasn't a snow shovel either. It was a coal scoop! And I dug with that. In fact, one day Chuck let me borrow the shovel and I was digging and it started to rain. I went right on digging in the rain because the rain softened the dirt a little bit. I was soaking wet when I went back to return the shovel. Chuck said, 'I watched you out there, and I couldn't believe what I was seeing! Why did you keep on working?' 'Because it was easier to dig, and I thought I might not get this shovel from you again,' I said."

An ambulance barged by, its siren blaring through the beeping of the bulldozer and the drone of the crane. On the top floor of the skeletal high-rise, several construction workers lifted their heads at the disturbance, their faces suddenly visible beneath their hard-hats. Marti showed us the third slide, wedging it between her thumb and index finger. In the picture it is early spring. Marti, in beige slacks and a rose-colored blouse, kneels in her garden picking weeds. A row of spinach edges the sidewalk a few feet away from a fire hydrant. In the center of the plot, Baskin Robbins ice cream containers surround and support tomato seedlings. Behind the tomatoes, netting covers rows of lettuce and peas. Pie pans and strips of tinfoil sparkle and flutter down from stakes hammered into the dirt.

"Because my new plot was closer to the sidewalk, the people with dogs walked them there. The dogs would run through my garden. They'd tear it up after I'd have it all planted and raked. There would be these huge paw prints the size of a baseball. Then they'd do their duty right smack in the middle of what I'd planted. So, I wrote this gardening publication and said, 'What can I do about these dog owners who let their animals run loose in my garden?'

"They published my letter, and you know, I got a stack of mail in reply. Some of the responses were absolutely insane. Somebody told me to build a hedge of blackberry bushes, and the thorns would keep the dogs from coming in. I don't know how they thought I was going to get blackberry bushes as tall as a hedge in the first place. This would have been a terrific endeavor—financially as well as practically. And I don't know how I would have gotten myself in and out.

"Of course, many of the letters said, 'Put up a fence.' Well, I wasn't allowed to put up a fence. It wasn't my property to fence. Then, some of the letters said, 'Use mothballs.' They suggested that dogs don't like the smell. But the mothballs didn't bother the dogs at all. They may have helped a bit with the rabbits and mice, but the dogs squatted right down beside them.

"Then somebody said, 'Red pepper.' Well, I tried that and it got to be expensive. Finally I found a little place, an Indian supply house, in Uptown. I bought red pepper by the five-pound sack and I sprinkled it around my garden. But the rain washed it away.

"Then one of the letters said, 'If you happen to be within reach of a zoo, you might try lion, tiger and big cat pooh.' Well, that was no problem. I just went over to Lincoln Park and made friends with the zookeeper. And after we got to know each other, I said, 'Will you save your lion and tiger pooh for me?' And he did. Then I went over with a huge garbage sack and a cart—not a wheelbarrow, but a grocery cart. I lined my cart with the garbage sack, and then I put smaller sacks inside. I got almost all the way home and I met this woman with a tiny white poodle. That dog was so interested in my sack of pooh, I thought, 'This is a bad omen.'

"When I got to my garden, I put chunks of that stuff wherever the dogs had been coming in, or had been using the garden for their private playground. And it just stank so! Worse than the dogs! It was terrible. And you know, the dogs loved it."

In the fourth slide it is early summer. A woman wearing blue jeans and a sleeveless yellow blouse stands in front of her garden, spraying water from a hose. Old paving bricks line the borders and create a round flower planter in the center of the plot where purple and white pansies are just beginning to blossom. Seed packets are tacked to stakes marking young rows of lettuce and corn. Outside the garden's perimeter, foxtail and quack grass billow up and run toward the sidewalk. A UPS truck is double-parked in front of the florist shop across the street.

"About this time, the two young men with the lamp shop, who originally organized the gardens, moved to the suburbs. Then a woman named Barbara took over. That's Barbara in this shot watering her flowers. She was a nurse who worked for Oscar Mayer."

We peered at the slide again, and several workers taking a break on a fourth-story beam waved. One of them unrolled a pack of cigarettes from his T-shirt sleeve. Another swigged a last drop of Coke, then sailed the can near the newly poured slab of concrete below.

Marti seemed oblivious. Her fingers, the nails painted with a clear polish, touched her shoulders, then danced around her chest, patting the V-neck of her dress. Her attention focused straight ahead, almost beyond us, as she fingered her necklace, each tiny seashell on the string. She brushed her bangs out of her eyes, then crossed her legs, redistributing her weight on the barrel.

"Barbara had a committee to help her, but as hard as she got after them, they didn't do very well. Finally, she married and moved to Detroit, and there I was. I had been one of Barbara's committee members and had taken care of helping collect the money in the beginning. No one else would do it and I wanted to garden. So I thought, All right, I'm stuck with it. I figured I might as well go ahead and run the gardens. And I did."

Each spring, Marti mapped out the plots and called all the previous year's gardeners, fifty by that time, for renewals. She hounded the tardy for their dues and with the money bought tools and equipment, including hoses, a specially fitted faceplate for the fire hydrant and a customized wrench from the city to open the main. Once the faceplate was attached, water flowed from the hydrant through two primary hoses that ran in op-

posite directions, then subdivided into two more hoses, spouting four nozzles in total.

"And who put it all out in the spring? I did! And the last one in the garden at night was supposed to shut off the water, and since I lived nearby, I'd often come over at dusk and the garden would be deserted and the water would still be on, the faceplate and everything attached. You were supposed to take this all apart and hide it under some shrubbery, because people stole the faceplates—they had to be replaced at great expense—and they stole the wrench. In fact, for two or three years, we got along with a wrench that I got from Walter, our building janitor. It was a regular monkey wrench, a huge one. But we wore the teeth off of it, so I went back to the city again through my alderman and got another wrench.

"For a while we stashed things at the florist shop across the street. But the trouble was, if it was after six o'clock at night, they'd be closed, so people wouldn't know where to put the wrench. And the shop didn't open until ten o'clock in the morning. Some people who went to work early wanted to water their garden, say, at seven-thirty, and they couldn't. And you had to water regularly because the soil dried out so fast. There was tremendous drainage. There had been a cellar under my plot and everything seeped right into it. So finally, we just gave up on storing things at the florist's.

"But, oh, stealing was a big problem! You didn't dare leave anything on that hydrant and walk away. You had to take it with you and put it right alongside your plot. Then, when you were through, you asked if anyone else in the garden wanted to water. If they did, you took them the stuff and said, 'Here, now when you're finished, you hide it.' And if they didn't hide it, we were out of luck.

"Oh, we had a lot of theft. See those beautiful flowers in Barbara's garden in the slide? Someone came along and dug up all the pansies. We had a man who lived in a high-rise nearby. He would stand on his balcony and look out and see people in the garden stealing. He had a megaphone and he'd shout, 'GET OUT OF THAT GARDEN! I'M THE POLICE!' They didn't know where the voice was coming from up there, and they'd leave. That was fine as long as Warren saw them, but he wasn't home all the time."

Marti, who sandwiched her outdoor work into an already busy schedule, couldn't stand sentinel in the garden, either. Even today, she is up at five A.M., exercises to a TV program from five-thirty to six, then jogs through Lincoln Park and returns home for a light breakfast. She likes to be at her writing desk by eight-thirty. When she gardened, she spent time in her plot between seven and eight o'clock. Then once her regular workday was complete and the glare from the afternoon sun too intense at the window over her desk for her to continue writing advertising copy, she would return to her vegetables.

Marti held the fifth slide up, a shot taking in the scale of the project, twenty or thirty gardens within view, all staked and marked off by low stone fences. The focal garden is divided into five raised beds—three free-form mounds of earth, then two rectangles contained within 1 × 10-foot pine boards. A hose slinks along a pathway in the foreground, and five tomato cages wrapped in plastic stand guard over the spring crops.

"I gradually learned not to dig too deep, because the deeper I went, the more brick and cement and old iron and junk I found. So, after I dug a lot of this up, I had about a foot of tillable soil and tried not to go below this. There were a couple of men who were very smart and made the raised beds shown in this slide. Those two raised-bed gardeners were very successful. One of them gave me my strawberry plants.

"Oh, there were all kinds of gardening theories. Some people believed in planting up on mounds with a kind of ditch between. Others created raised beds with railroad ties. And some people gardened on trellises. I never held to any of the theories, though. I just planted my seedlings. I never had any training, so I just did what it said on the seed packet or in my gardening magazine."

But whatever the planting method, all the Old Town gardens had the same pest problems, the soil too poor to allow the seedlings much resistance to infestation. During her nine years of gardening, Marti never stopped battling the intruders. She cut out squash vine borers from the roots of zucchini, then reset the plants. And she placed little saucers of beer all over her plot in hopes of drowning the slugs. "Wasted an awful lot of beer that way, and most of the slugs crawled right by the traps."

Birds pulled corn seedlings out of the ground, so most of the gardeners gave up on that crop. But Marti attached strands of aluminum foil to stakes and mounted old cans on top of poles to flicker and scare away the pests. She was successful, too. By the end of July, she could usually count on lunches of fresh sweet corn. And then for the first few years, the rabbits nibbled off Marti's carrots, lettuce and peas. She finally began covering the plants with homemade netting.

"I used to save this net that grapefruit comes in. I'd take these bags and lay them out flat. Then I got yarn and sewed them together so that I had big long strips of netting. I put it over the plants that were just coming up, where the rabbits sneak in and chew. Then later, when my strawberries were ripe, I put the netting over the berries because the birds used to feast on those, too."

To protect her Swiss chard, Marti rode the bus to Baskin Robbins and brought home ice cream containers. She cut out the bottoms, then sank the cartons in a ring around her greens, letting the sun in, but keeping the rabbits out. "It looked terrible, like you were growing ice cream containers, but it worked very well."

In her nine years of gardening, Marti's only real crop failure was watermelon. Her soil was just too heavy. "I read that melons need sandy soil, so I tried to add sand to my plot. I even went to the beach and dragged home buckets full. And sand weighs a lot. Then, whenever I'd see a construction site, I'd stop and ask, 'May I please have a bucket of your sand?' They'd think I was nuts, but I'd go get a bucket or two, and I'd haul the sand home to make my melon patch. I never did get any watermelons, although I tried so hard. But I did get some quite good cantaloupe."

In the sixth slide, an Asian-American family—father, mother and teenage daughter—are working their plot. Half of the space is tilled, the other half overgrown with weeds. In the center of the shot, the man bends over a shovel, turning the soil, while beside him the woman rakes through debris and breaks up the large clumps of dirt. Behind them, her hands in white gardening gloves, the daughter stoops to lift out bricks and chunks of concrete.

"We all had to struggle with our gardens so much at first. It took me four years before my asparagus was ready because I didn't have any more sense than to plant it by the fence in the shade. But once I had it, it was just wonderful. And I had strawberries. My bed produced loads of strawberries, big, lovely berries, that I mostly gave away. The only trouble was, I had to pick them, and that's backbreaking hot work. I did it usually in the morning when it was cooler. I'd saved a lot of those green baskets you get at the grocery, and I asked my friends to save theirs. I had bunches of those things. I'd fill them full, stack them one on top of the other in grocery sacks, and carry them home."

In addition to doling out strawberries to her friends, Marti bartered with other gardeners for samples of their bounty. With the Asian-American family she traded berries for Chinese cabbage and pak-choi, then eventually began growing Asian vegetables herself to create even more variety in her own plot. "As a child, because of my father's garden, I had learned to eat all different varieties of vegetables—eggplant, Swiss chard and spinach—things most children don't eat. And as an adult, I just kept experimenting. I'd go over to my Asian friends and say, 'What's that?' and they'd give me a bunch of greens and tell me how to cook them. I liked the taste of those vegetables so much, I finally bought packets of seeds to sow myself."

Over the years, through tool and equipment sharing and common struggle, the Old Town gardeners developed a sense of community and began to hold picnics at the end of each summer. To pay for the festivities, they used the money left over from their annual dues—once they had deducted expenses for replacing all the leaking hoses, broken shovels and stolen wrenches.

"Barbara was still in charge when we inaugurated our picnics. So she bought hot dogs wholesale from Oscar Mayer. Then she bought some buns and beer. Those who lived nearby and had grills brought those, and we would have cookouts. After Barbara moved, I was in charge and had no

access to Oscar Mayer. So we all brought our own meat. I would bring beer and potato chips, cheese puffs, soft drinks for the children. That was fun! And then, of course, we'd have strawberries for dessert."

Marti's strawberries were bearing when the developer bulldozed the lot in 1984 to begin work on his high-rise. For nine years, while they gardened the ground, beginning in the rubble and hardpan, the neighborhood had fought the city council over zoning. They lost, and then fought, and then lost again in the courts. "By that time, the developers were very angry with us. They thought, All right. The gardeners are against us. We'll show them. So they ripped up our gardens. They just plowed everything down, the whole garden, everything. That was in June, when the plants were just beginning to come up. Then the developers left this land blank for three years."

Marti sighed and swiveled around on the barrel to glance back over her shoulder at the construction site. Two men, balanced on a tenth-story beam, waited to receive a load from the crane. The forklift lumbered across the bare ground now, carting plywood, stirring dust into the air, while a man in an orange hard-hat directed the machine's forks around piles of concrete block and mounds of sand.

Marti's fingers fluffed the curls around her face, then moved to the V-neck of her dress, where she patted her hint of cleavage. Tiny, pale, the skin on her fingers finely wrinkled, she looked fragile, a wisp of a woman surrounded by machinery and building materials, her sibilant voice nearly drowned by the din of construction and street traffic. Yet Marti Roynon is anything but fragile. She is a survivor, capable of strapping her first pair of wooden skis onto her feet during her honeymoon at Sun Valley or whisking down the most dangerous pass on Baldy Mountain, or of buying a pair of skates and working with her husband, a passionate winter athlete, to become a figure-skating champion. Even today, at an age when most people would have retired, Marti continues to work a full schedule writing copy and conducting photographic sessions for her freelance advertising business. The state of Washington, which hired her to promote apples, was one of her most recent clients. And last Christmas found Marti once again on the slopes in Aspen. For Marti, although loss is real, it never brings defeat.

"After Jack died, the year before I even had the garden, I just scrubbed floors on my hands and knees. In grief, you need to do something physical. Then when I got my plot, I dug instead of scrubbed. Gardening is just a great release. I worked very long and hard at it. I dug and hoed and used the pitchfork. Then after my son died so suddenly, I just dug all the harder."

# Reunion

## An Interview with Floyd Brannon

*I was born and raised in Wilson, Oklahoma. But I left there in 1953 to come to Galesburg, Illinois. My brother was working at Butler Manufacturing Company. I was a machinist and fork-lift operator. Worked there until my retirement. In Oklahoma, I always helped in my family's garden. But I began my own garden in 1953. You know, just to see if I could grow things. I been gardening ever since. I used to garden every morning for a couple of hours before I went to the factory. Now, I'm still out in one of my two gardens every morning at six. I have four daughters and they don't garden. They do come out and watch me, then pick and eat.*

—Floyd Brannon, Galesburg, Illinois

At five-thirty A.M., Floyd Brannon's Galesburg, Illinois, neighborhood was almost deserted. The sun rose over the smokestacks of the Butler Manufacturing Company a few blocks away. A boy zigzagged back and forth across the street, pitching Galesburg's *Register Mail* onto stoops and front porches, his canvas bag sagging below his knees. A flock of sparrows chittered as they landed, first on Floyd's old riding mower, with the harrow he had attached to the back, then on the rusted tiller in his yard.

The front door of Floyd's bungalow creaked open. Moved from another lot a few years earlier, the house was without a foundation, the four corners propped on cement blocks, the center sagging. For several minutes, the door with its torn screen remained ajar, then Floyd shuffled out in his stocking feet, a roadster cap cocked over his eyes. He lowered himself onto the top step and patted his shirt pocket for a pack of Pall Malls. Gray sideburns trailed from his hairline, and a thin mustache dotted his upper lip. The cleft on his chin was fleshy, extended by a scar that wavered, then cut straight across to the edge of his jaw. Veins snaked up his hands and arms, disappearing near his elbows under the hems of his sleeves.

"You girls looking for me, I bet. I knew you coming around sometime. I kept asking the neighbors if they seen two girls wanting to talk to me about gardening. But it's been two weeks."

Floyd Brannon is a hard man to find. The front door of his squat white house is always locked, the shades pulled. And Floyd is usually not around. Neighbors say to try the tavern. His daughter, who lives just around the corner, says to look in the garden, the one at the other end of Holton Street—but early in the morning. Only insomniacs catch Floyd *before* he sets to work, sauntering up the middle of the street, then weaving through a maze of backyards—under clotheslines, around doghouses with German shepherds on the stake and, finally, through chain-link gates—to his half-acre of vegetables, where he often labors from six to eight, tilling, planting and cultivating crops which he leaves for his ex-wife and daughters to reap.

"I don't eat none of that stuff. But I been tilling this land for thirty-five years, ever since I came to Illinois from Wichita, Kansas, in 1953 to work at Butler's. My brothers was all working out there, so I came, too. Drove a forklift. But I learned to garden way before that. In Oklahoma, where I was raised on a farm."

An unlit Pall Mall dangled from Floyd's mouth, several stray wisps of

*Floyd Brannon*

tobacco poking out. His lips hardly moved when he spoke. A shy man whose face and voice withhold expression, Floyd talks with his hands—not in gestures that underscore his speech, but in the ritual motions of a smoker, flicking the lighter, cupping the flame, slipping the cigarette between index and middle finger. With his roadster cap slung low, he looked like a jazz musician, a Pall Mall the instrument which he played on every register.

"But, oh, I didn't learn too much from home. See, my dad passed when I was only nine years old. I seen my mother and them working, but I never did garden until I started my plot here. I suppose I remember some stuff—like mixing up that arsenic and water to put on the potatoes to drive away them big speckled bugs. We used to take a mop, dip it in the stuff and sprinkle that on the plants. But I don't use that no more. Don't grow potatoes here. Too much digging.

"Yeah. I plant my garden. But I don't do much else. You know, I cultivate the ground some, get the seedbed ready with my tillers over there. But I don't use no fertilizer or nothing. Now back in Oklahoma, my dad did that. Not pig droppings. That smelled too much. And not mule, neither. Too many weed seeds. But chicken droppings was good. 'Course, you had to let it sit out for a while. Put those directly on the ground and it burn everything up. But around here, the ground's rich enough. Now this guy back of me, he takes and puts fertilizer down his rows. But there's one thing about that stuff. If the ground is rich, and you put fertilizer in, then all it's gonna do is make a big vine on your plant. Won't be no vegetable or nothing else on there. So I don't put nothing. Just plant the seeds and let them go."

Floyd hunched on the stoop, his eyes, filmed over and bloodshot, fixed on a spot across the street. Even when he drew on his cigarette, his cheeks remained slack, the skin falling from temple to chin in a single sheet.

"Like I said, I don't do much. Don't water, neither. I say, 'The good Lord sends the rain down, and that's the way the ground's supposed to get wet.' If water's convenient, then I wouldn't mind using it. But I don't have a hookup in my garden up there. 'Course, if I did water, I wouldn't put water right on the plants. I'd just take it down the middle of the row. Water around here's got something in it. Put it right on top of the leaves, it's damaging. Leaves get rusty.

"Yeah. The guy next to my lot up the street waters his beans using coffee cans in the ground. He punched some holes in the cans, then he sank them down next to the beans. Did that 'cause his beans about burned up. He figured when it rained, the water wouldn't run off. You know, it would seep out of the can and down around the roots instead. But them cans ain't no good, either. Beans still burned. Water ain't going to last that long. The ground's so dry now, it just soaks up all the water in the can in ten minutes. That guy's beans look poorer than mine. In my opinion, what he did is worse than not giving them no water at all."

Floyd sparked his lighter, then sucked in five long draws, the smoke floating past his eyes and the beak of his cap toward the rusted mailbox listing from a nail above his head.

"Water or don't water. One's just about as bad as another. Same thing with planting carrots and lettuce. You get them too deep, they can't come through. Get them too shallow, they won't come up. Some people put a board over to keep them wet. But the guy down the block did that and forgot about it. The seeds all dried up and he didn't get no carrots.

"Now I never have no trouble with beans. And if it don't rain, I'm gonna plant some more tomorrow. Get them out of South Dakota, and I know those'll come up. Not like the ones from out at the dealer here in town. Don't like them bush beans anyhow. I got a whole row of pole beans and I just let them run on the ground. Too much work to stick them up on poles.

"And I never buy much of anything in town. Lot of nurseries got some kind of spray they put on them plants to make them grow. But as soon as you get them home and in the ground, the things'll quit on you. Oh, I buy transplants sometimes, but I can tell by looking if it's been sprayed. Plant's got more bigger leaves. And they're real timid. You know, if you fool around with the vine, the leaves are brittle and they'll break right off. I got some plants from a guy out here at the mall. He told me, 'Man, we got some pretty ones.' And I said, 'They ain't no count. They been sprayed.' And he said, 'Well, you go out there and try some.' I did and I got some peppers from another place where they hadn't been sprayed, and I planted them together. I didn't get nothing off them sprayed plants. But the others had so many peppers they could hardly hold themselves up."

A clump of ash broke off from the cigarette in Floyd's mouth and fell onto the cement.

"This year, I done sold about eight bushels of beans. 'Course, when I pick them beans, I do as the book says: 'If it's too wet or heavy dew, don't pick.' Before I got ahold of that book, we was just picking anytime, but I think it damaged the vines. The beans stopped blooming on me.

"Yeah. And some people want tomatoes. Since I been retired, they all know I have the garden. So, some of them want ten or twelve, and some want a bushel. It depends. I had some this summer as big as saucers. Delicious tomatoes, I call them. I don't think you're gonna find one of them Big Boys no bigger than that."

Floyd stroked a fresh Pall Mall, his fingers feathering the tip, then sliding up and down the translucent paper, the cigarette rotating slowly in his palm.

"Now, when you pick the tomatoes, that depends, too. If it's dry, you take them off the vine a little early, before they get real red. Too many on there, the vine don't have enough moisture to bring to them all, and it'll stop blooming. If you take those tomatoes off early, the vine can go on producing more. But if it's raining regular, it don't make no difference when you pick. My tomatoes here, they ain't had nothing on them. No more than the good Lord watered.

"And every year now I'm asked for okra. I first had some here I guess

three years ago. Ordered the seeds from Gurney. At the local dealer, they say, 'We don't get that stuff. It don't sell.' I told him, 'Well, if you don't got it, naturally it won't sell. People don't know about it.'

"Okra grow real good around here. I just took my seeds and throwed them out. Didn't think it was gonna do nothing. But it come up and just growed wild. Then I took some over to the tavern one Saturday and asked if anybody wanted it. At first, they said, 'No.' Most of them didn't even know what the stuff was. 'What is that?' they asked. 'How do you cook it?' I told them, dice it up, and my mother, she just put it in a skillet and fried it. But now they got them deep-fat fryers. Nobody knew nothing about no deep-fat fryer when I was growing up. Or you can just boil it in clear water, and put salt and pepper on.

"'Course, me, I don't like okra. But I can tell you, the red is better than the green. Same taste, but the red produces more. I got one row of red and two of green up there. All planted the same day and come up the same time. But my wife and daughters they been done harvesting red okra for a long time. And the green just now's starting to put on."

Okra wasn't the only vegetable Floyd's ex-wife and daughters were harvesting. Up in the garden three blocks away, despite Galesburg's month-long drought, the women, white towels wrapped around their necks to catch the sweat, stooped over bushelbaskets brimming with cucumbers.

The mother and two daughters, all wearing sunglasses, blue slacks and white blouses, bent and picked, rising to mop their faces, then bending once more, their backs curving in unison. As soon as the baskets were filled, the women lugged them toward a Chinese elm that shaded one quadrant of the garden, and grabbed more containers which they began piling with blazing red plump tomatoes. Nearby, an old washtub overflowed with green beans. Although no one spoke, a current of sympathy laced the air.

"Morning's kind of like a family reunion up here. But I plant and they pick. I can tell you one thing. Whenever the beans come on, I be someplace else. But I always be here to put the seeds in the ground."

Floyd guided us along a section of cow peas, snapping off a pod and rubbing it between his fingers. "You can just let these dry on the vine, then some will come up again every year. I give them the same service I give everybody. But because I don't have to replant them all the time, it don't take that much to do it. 'Course, if you want a green pea, then you got to take them out of the shuck. You get them that way when they're half-grown and they're just like green beans. You can can those, or freeze them. Either way.

"When we's on the farm in Oklahoma, we come out in the evening this time of the year, we'd have to go pick peas. Bring them in and let them dry some, then we take them off the vine, put them in a sack, and whupped them. Sometimes there'd be two hundred pounds of them peas. We never did eat all that stuff.

"And back in them days, we made scarecrows. Took a couple of sticks and nailed it together in the shape of a cross. Then we put on a man's shirt and pants, old pair of overalls. Next, we'd stuff them. Put a big straw hat on its head. But we wouldn't give him no face. Just the hat. Then we stuck him up. Wind would move the clothes and chase the birds away.

"And see them cantaloupe down there? They's big as my fist, but the vine's already dead. The grubs got them. Now the grubs so bad, I didn't plant no watermelon this year. 'Course, you need sandy ground for them things to grow. You can add sand, but you got to get the right kind. The sand you get down here at one of these cement places, that ain't nothing but rock. It ain't no good putting that in. It ain't going to mix with the other soil. It's just going to sit out there and won't grow nothing on it. If you want sand, you got to go around Oquawka. That's about sixteen miles from

here. They got all kinds of fish there on that river. Catfish, perch, big bass. Yeah, you want sand, you go down to that river. You go down to one of these concrete places, there won't nothing grow in your ground.

"See, this guy right there on Knox Street, he went down to the cement company and bought two pickup loads of sand. Then he mixed it in his garden. But it ain't doing no good, because it wasn't nothing but rock. I told him, 'Man, you got to get to Oquawka and buy you some of that sand.' But he wouldn't listen. And where he put that sand from the cement company, won't nothing grow. He know that now. He even had a guy come and plow it real deep, trying to get that sand way down below where it wouldn't do no harm. But half the stuff what he plants, even if it come up, it don't grow."

At the far end of the garden, the women had reached the five-foot-high okra, its leaves forming a canopy over the beans and cucumbers. With paring knives, they sliced the vegetables from their stems and dropped the pods into five-gallon galvanized pails hanging from the crooks of their arms. Beyond the women, the garden straggled off into a tangle of dandelions and crab grass toward the street, where the houses thinned into the outskirts of town and the playground of a boarded-up school sat empty in the heat.

"I got something to tell you. Take a bottle. Any kind of fruit jar or pop bottle, and put it down right in the row. Do that and them critters ain't gonna eat your greens. Now, a lot of people take these old pie pans and hang them up on stakes. But that rabbit'll go right up there to them pans, and pretty soon, he don't pay no heed. He go right on in there and he eat up everything.

"And like you got some coons stealing your corn. Spread newspaper down between the rows. Them coons come and step on that, and the noise is enough to scare them off. And I know a guy up at the tavern, he say he go to the beauty parlor and gets him some hair to put in the toe of an old pair of hose. Ties that on a stake, and he say it keeps the critters away. I never tried it, so maybe it's no count. And somebody else say it even scares the deer.

"'Course, down in Oklahoma we didn't have no coons in our garden. We had all them dogs. Once my daddy had him a good one named Ugly. That Ugly howled so much no critter come near our place. Howled all day and howled all night. 'Cept one time, my dad stayed away too long. He went out with Ugly and some other guys into the woods. And I don't know what they done out there, but they stayed all night. And when they come home in the morning, Ugly ran straight for the corn. Started howling and sniffing, sniffing and howling. He didn't find no coon, but he didn't find no corn, either. While Dad and Ugly was out hunting their coon in the woods, another whole family moved into the garden and they had themselves one good meal.

"Another guy, he's got an old radio stuck in a trash can in the middle of his corn. Leaves it playing all night. And he ain't had no critters all summer long. Trouble is, you got to come out here and turn that thing on.

"Lots what people say, I don't know if they's true. Some people tell, 'Don't plant nothing near the walnut tree. There's something in the roots that poisons the plants.' Other people say, 'Don't plant your tomatoes in the same ground for too long, else they get a virus and curl up.'

"Then, a lady up the street here, she have green peas. I don't grow them 'cause you got to tie them up. Too much work. And she say, one day them birds come down and stole all her peas. Every last one gone. But I tell her I got all these berries and the birds don't bother them none. Now, I seen them crows, way down yonder at Oquawka, where they have that small grain. I seen a bunch of them birds going in there. Some of them guys say they have crows awful. So bad, in the fall everything's gone.

"But I tell that lady I ain't seen no crows around here. 'Must be you live in a better part of town.' But she said she was sure it was them birds. I didn't believe her no count. I know birds, and they don't never pick one vine clean. She said, 'I'm going to be sure this won't happen again.' She put out a scarecrow, pie tins and I don't know what all.

"Then she said them birds didn't give her no more trouble. But just the other day she come down here and tell me, 'You know, it wasn't the birds after all that was stealing my peas. It was the boys next door. Their mother made them come over and apologize.'"

By now the women's pails were half-filled with okra, the pods, thin purple fingers, silhouetted against the matte finish of the galvanized metal. A swallowtail butterfly landed on a thistle and spread its black-and-yellow wings. The German shepherd at the edge of the plot growled at a beagle that had strayed into the yard. Floyd leaned against an old tiller, his brown oxfords filmed with dust. He might have been posing for a Walker Evans photograph, one hand stuck in the pocket of his baggy pants, just the two middle buttons still clinging to his shirt. He talked while the women picked, their backs to him, his speech infused with the rhythm of their bending and straightening.

"But I'll tell you something sure. If you plant a bean in the morning—and keep this in mind—the first blooms come on those beans, is gonna fall off. Don't plant beans in the morning. This is a sure thing.

"And corn, you don't want to grow too tall. That ain't no good corn. 'Cause a tall stalk ain't gonna get no good ears. You go out there in the country in those cornfields, and you see a lot of corn taller than I am. Then you see some other corn is low. Low corn, better stuff, was planted in the dark of the moon. I know, lots of people say the other way around. But that ain't right. You listen to me. In the dark of the moon, you plant everything that's producing on top of the ground. Like beans, peas, collards, tomatoes, cabbage, them types of things. But not like potatoes. They's an underground plant. Them you plant in the light of the moon. When the moon's growing, then your plant will be a-growing, too.

"That works for a lot of things, but trouble is you got to know when they was started. Like if you go buy a tomato or a cabbage transplant at the store, you don't know when they planted it. So, you can't plan. You can set it out by the moon, but that don't say it's gonna go.

"Back in Oklahoma, I remember my dad talking. You plant corn, and

cotton and potatoes and stuff that way. He wouldn't plant nothing like corn without looking at the moon. He say, 'If the corn's way up high, you can't hardly reach it.' And they did the same with pigs and cows and things. You know, cow give birth, and you take that calf away according to the moon.

"One thing I don't put no stock by. A lot of people say, with potatoes you got to put them in on Good Friday. Some people even tell you with the eye up so they can see to get out. I bet you I ain't planted potatoes in my whole life twice on no Good Friday. So it don't mean nothing to it. But the moon, there ain't no question to that."

Floyd's family began consolidating the harvest under the elm, dumping all the cucumbers into one large basket, the tomatoes, cow peas, okra and collards into others. One daughter drove the old blue Chevy onto the grass. Then, forming an assembly line, the three women loaded the car, the ex-wife and first daughter slinging bushelbaskets on their hips, the second daughter cradling them and wedging them into the trunk.

Back on his stoop, Floyd fished in his pocket for a fresh cigarette. By now, the neighborhood was awake. Across the street, a woman in pink curlers pried the *Register Mail* from the branches of a spreading yew, her spotted terrier yapping at her feet. Two doors down, Floyd's neighbor revved his LawnBoy. Three adolescents whipped by on dirt bikes, their radios leaving a wake of reggae.

"See all them vegetables they picked today. That'll keep them busy canning and freezing. Feed them all winter long. But not me. I don't like any of it. I just garden because I like to grow things. We don't need that garden there. It ain't a necessity. I get up at five o'clock in the morning anyway. And if I didn't garden, I'd just have to mow that grass. I guess gardening's just a habit I take up. Even when I was still working, I was doing the same thing. And I know I can't just sit around now that I'm retired. I heard about a guy, he stopped working and he started talking to himself. Now he goes around town, and nobody can understand a word he say.

"And then there's another guy right across the street here. He retired and he just sat. He ain't older than I am, but now he can't hardly walk. He can't hardly see to drive. He just messed up. I know he didn't used to *do* nothing. And now he *can't* do nothing.

"Lot of my friends used to say, 'Man, how do you do all that? Working in the garden, then working in the factory, then working in the garden at night.' Well, I tell them, 'It ain't so much that it has to be done. I might just go up there and walk around or pull a weed.' Yeah, I say, gardening ain't no necessity. I do it because I want to."

And Floyd wants to garden every morning. Unless he walks up the street and steps onto the ground he has tilled for thirty-five years, his day has no beginning. Worse, he has no life. It is as if he is nourished, not by eating what he grows, but by growing it in the first place. And if Floyd and his wife are separated, their daughters now in homes of their own, each spring they recreate the family, Floyd by sowing, the women by reaping.

The only morning Floyd didn't tend his garden that season, he drove the fifty miles to Flint's Soul Food in Rock Island, Illinois, to pick up baby back ribs, spareribs, chicken and sausage for a family reunion. That evening, in his daughter's backyard, the air heavy with the smell of citronella candles and minted iced tea, he passed the time eating ribs, talking fishing and reflecting on the drought. Whenever relatives asked if he were worried about his garden in the dry spell, Floyd would draw on his Pall Mall, his tapered fingers forming a gentle arc over his mouth, and tell his aunt from Tulsa, his brother from Joplin, or his cousin from Wichita, "No, I ain't worried. I ain't worried no count. I just let the good Lord water."

# 3    Beauty and Bounty

We tried to live back East a few years ago when we started having children. Both families are back there, Pennsylvania and Virginia. We gardened there, but it was never quite right. It just didn't look like it should have. The soil was red. We said, "This soil will never grow anything. No way, this red stuff." So we didn't stay. And the exhilarating thing about returning to this part of the country was the aesthetics of seeing the black dirt—especially after it rained.—CONSTANCE KINGSTON, *Lincoln, Nebraska*

I've never been able to sleep late. Too many years of nursing. So I'm up early. It's the most beautiful time of the day—to watch the morning come. The day is fresh, and new, and maybe it will have great things. To see the flowers open and the birds arrive, the clouds break. There's just something about morning that's renewal. Some of this must come from my mother. She taught us the names of all the flowers and birds. I don't know how she knew them. She read a lot, I guess. She saw so much beauty in everything.

—HELEN WESTON, *Topeka, Kansas*

When my first husband and I bought this house, there wasn't a thing planted on the whole acre and a half, except those maples and that large lilac. Actually, the whole back section was just part of a field. I planted all the evergreens, spaded out all the gardens by hand. A lot of sweat and probably a few pounds shed! But the visions of all those roses and morning glories, all the rows of broccoli and tomatoes, the rhubarb jam on my shelves, inspired me to go on.—JENNIFER TRAPP, *Salem, Wisconsin*


Sarge, tell them how you know when you can plant in the spring.

Depends on the weather. Every year's different.

Oh, tell them about how you take the soil in your hand the way you do. Tell them about how it feels.

Well, when I want to see if the ground's ready, I take some dirt in my hands—like this. And if it crumbles, if it's black and loose, if it's mellow, then I know that I can till. And if it's muddy, I know that I have to wait. Have no choice. Once I plant, though, and things start growing, my work's done. I can just sit back and let nature take care of everything.

—MARION AND SARGE WENDLANDT, *Iowa City, Iowa*

# Beauty and Bounty

## An Interview with Carl Klaus

*My Aunt Ada's three-vegetable dinners, my Uncle Norman's country picnics, my Uncle Roy's Victory garden, my Uncle Manny's Saturday morning grocery sprees, and my Aunt Celia's mesh shopping bag bulging with broccoli and cauliflower from the West Side Market—these memories from my depression-era childhood in Cleveland, Ohio, remind me that though I was orphaned at the age of five, I never thought of myself as such, because my aunts and uncles and cousins never let me go hungry. Food, good food of all kinds, was a major part of their lives and thus of mine and my brother Marshall's—a way of knowing that someone cared. So I have tried to carry on that tradition—and pass it on to my children—in the gardens I have tended, the dills I have pickled, and the dinners I have cooked. I've been gardening and pickling and cooking for thirty-five years—as a graduate student in English at Cornell University, as an instructor at Bowdoin College, and as a professor of one sort or another at the University of Iowa. At all of these places I've found that in good food good things converge.*

*—Carl Klaus, Iowa City, Iowa*

"If you had been here about three to four weeks ago, this garden would have knocked your eyes out! The peas were all still pendant," Carl Klaus rhapsodized, his arms swooping out toward both ends of his vegetable plot, where the plants were laid out within a 44 × 22-foot brick frame to create an elegant tapestry of texture and color—from the blue-green of the broccoli and cauliflower leaves on either end, to the slick golden skin of the peppers and the hairy foliage of the French Cornichon cucumbers in the middle. "But the garden's still beautiful." Carl stepped back and squinted. His soft brown eyes took in the sweep of the vegetables from behind tortoise-shell-rimmed bifocal glasses.

Carl is a professor of English at the University of Iowa, but his passion for gardening is as much a part of his local reputation as are his eight textbooks on prose style, the teaching of writing, and the essay. Even more than that, gardening is the force around which everything else in Carl's life coalesces, the one activity embracing the physical, the emotional and the intellectual. If Carl writes articulately and convincingly about prose style, he communicates equally well the thrill of producing a perfect cauliflower.

"Let me explain my design to you. The space is divided into three sections. Here's one spring garden on the east, about ten to eleven feet of shell peas, cauliflower and onions. And on the west, there's another spring garden, the same size, of chives, beets, broccoli and snow peas. Then, in the middle, you have the summer garden, twenty-two feet, all mulched with straw, sloping from north to south. Here we grow nine tomato plants in the back, then two staggered rows of peppers, with the taller peppers in the rear, then cucumbers and cherry tomatoes. And of course, along the front, I raise my three varieties of lettuce. But I had to pull them up early this year because of the heat."

As he spoke, Carl's fingers worked the air in intricate patterns, fluttering and zigzagging as if he were weaving a brocade. On his head perched a high-crowned straw hat with a large, supple brim that flopped down over his forehead, stopping just short of his bushy brown eyebrows. His seersucker shirt fell in soft folds over his trim chest, and was tucked into a pair of beige shorts. That afternoon Carl was also wearing an old pair of huaraches instead of his usual gardening shoes—sneakers which one of his daughters had embroidered with a pair of butterflies on the toes. The grass, brown and brittle from lack of rain, crunched under his feet whenever he

*Carl Klaus*

shifted his weight to add clout to what he was saying or to help us view the garden from a subtly different perspective.

"The point of all this is, if you step back, what you see is a garden that's balanced. When the peas are in full growth, they're twenty-eight to forty inches high so that everything slopes out to create resolution at each end, not too abrupt, though. And the colors balance, too. The peas match each other, of course, and the two kinds flower simultaneously. That way we have the green foliage and the white flowers going north and south in the east and west spring gardens. Then we have the bluish green of the broccoli matching the bluish green of the cauliflower leaves. And the purple of the beets matches the red onions." Carl let his hands drift to his sides. "One year, I actually had red chard at one end to match the beets at the other. Now that was the perfect correspondence. But the trouble was, the chard interfered with my clustering the onions."

Carl plants, cultivates and appraises his garden much the way he reads and critiques the graduate theses of his students at the university—word for word, as well as cover to cover. When describing his garden, he begins with the whole, then gradually narrows his focus to the individual plants—the Supersonic and Ultra Boy tomatoes in the back row, the golden, four-lobed Quadrato D'Oro peppers toward the front, the Mr. Society onions off to one side. As he talks, his hands continuing their intricate movements, he fleshes out his vision to anyone who is interested, inviting them to view the garden through his eyes.

"Form, pattern and symmetry are all very important to me. See, in the center is the summer garden, which runs east and west and has the same slope and resolution as the two spring gardens. As you can see, the tomatoes are in the back because they are the tallest plants. Always put your tallest vegetables along the north end so they don't shade everything else. Next come our peppers, with the two tallest varieties in the center and in the back. I must always have everything balanced. What I want," Carl explained, lifting his arms again, elbows leading, like a conductor interpreting a musical score, "is for the viewer to look both up and out, from the cherry tomato in the front center to the larger tomatoes in the back. The vegetables are actually planted in a V-shape. On either side are the cucumbers, the French Cornichons. And if you're wondering what that is over there," he said, pointing to a rambling vine off to the side, "that's a squash. It's a rogue.

It came up on its own, and I always let something in here volunteer. There has to be a flaw in the design, you know."

Just then a male cardinal, a streak of red, dived down onto the lawn from the pin oak in the northwest corner of the yard. The bird hopped around on the oat-colored grass for several seconds, picking its way through a small pile of lawn debris, then winged back up into the tree, its color now barely visible behind the flush of dark green leaves. On the other side of the yard, a chickadee piped an insistent *fee-bee, fee-bee* from the limb of a robust Norway maple. It was four o'clock in the afternoon, the heat of the day just beginning to subside.

"There's something else I have to tell you. I'm so fussy about the design of my garden that I plant with a ruler. There's no other way. If you want symmetry, you have to measure. I even harvest in a manner to maintain the symmetry as long as possible. But I don't want you to misunderstand. The way I go about things is also functional. For example, my row of green onion sets is planted double thick. Then what I do is harvest every other onion, which leaves the remaining onions enough width to swell. And then, right up front here, I had my lettuces. They ran from the beginning of the west pea row to the beginning of the east pea row. I had eighteen lettuces in a perfectly symmetrical order. There were three kinds: ruby, which is completely purple and picks up the purple in the onions and beets; buttercrunch; and romaine. And I had the romaine in the center because they're the tallest. Then, on each side of the romaine, there were two or three rubies. And on each side of the rubies, there was buttercrunch. So the pattern was green/purple/green. And the trick is to harvest so that I keep the color balance as long as possible." Carl leaned over toward the edge of his garden, the rim of his hat casting his face in shadow, his glasses slipping down the bridge and along the curve of his nose. "Imagine the lettuce still here," he said, marking a small furrow in the damp dark soil with his index finger. "Then you can get a better idea how the brick border functions. When we bought the property, my wife, Kate, found the perfect spot for the garden, and even before we dug the plot, we decided to lay brick around the perimeter."

The contractor who built the Klauses' burnt red, two-story brick Victorian on top of a hill overlooking the golden dome of the former Iowa state capitol had been a brickmaker. He had had the house constructed for his own family one season when business was slow and his crew had no other projects to work on. Apparently he hadn't worried about waste. Once the Klauses had moved in and completed the interior renovations—stripping and restaining the original oak floors and woodwork, remodeling the kitchen, camouflaging the steam radiators—they turned their attention to the backyard and discovered bricks strewn everywhere. According to Carl, it was inevitable that Kate, always innovative with materials, would incorporate the bricks into the garden. "She just automatically started laying a border of bricks. And then for some reason, I ended up finishing the job. And somehow, somewhere in the process, the bricks inspired me like a frame. I could hardly wait to get a pleasing picture growing inside of it. And then, as an extension of that principle, I decided that what I had to do was to get vegetables to come out of that frame in a pleasing form as well. Beauty is really important to me."

Carl's next sentence was drowned out by the drone of an airplane drifting over the Klauses' yard, from the twenty-foot-long perennial bed Kate Klaus cultivates at one end of the property to the sunken limestone and cement patio abutting the house at the other end, the noise fading over the roof, where it finally blended with the hum of Iowa City traffic down below.

"Even as a child, I was struck by the beauty of vegetables. I used to go to the West Side Market in Cleveland once a week with my aunt, and the vegetables there really took my breath away. I don't know if it was that they were so good when my aunt cooked them, or that they were sold by those middle-European immigrants who were so ruddy and rosy-cheeked. Perhaps it was just the size of the vegetables themselves."

Orphaned when they were very young, Carl and his brother, Marshall, were raised by a series of relatives—first by one, then another set of older aunts and uncles, who all died, and then a cousin (old enough to be Carl's father) who had children Carl's age. It was the first aunt who included Carl in her expeditions to the West Side Market, an enclosed square block crammed with booths and vendors, thick with pungent smells, strange words and exotic shapes. But even then it was the sight of the vegetables— the waxy purple of the eggplants, the pale green of the cabbages, the deep lobes of the peppers—that most impressed Carl, the serious eight-year-old boy who hovered at his aunt's side as she shopped. And the sight of the vegetables and their bounty are what he recalls most intensely today.

"I can remember going back to Cleveland in 1971 to see my brother and visiting the West Side Market. Once again what struck me was the beauty of the place. And the vegetables were so large! I was able to buy a crate of mushrooms that were two or three inches in diameter, and the cauliflower I bought there were just as big as the ones I grow in my own garden.

"But I don't want you to think that I grow just for size. When most people think about vegetable gardening, they think only about bounty. They think about harvesting and eating the vegetables. It never occurs to them that vegetables are as beautiful as any plant or shrub or growing thing. But even beyond the beauty of the vegetable is the beauty of the plants. And that's something that we rarely hear about. I'm talking specifically about color, texture, shape and the growing habit. So I try to grow vegetables in a way that's going to realize as fully as possible the beauty of the whole. Now, what that means to me is that I would never put a tomato plant within a cage, for example. That would be an offense. It would be an offense to the plant, and ultimately to productivity. And this is something that I've come to understand in the seventeen years that I've been gardening. If you grow the plants in a way that's going to realize their fullest beauty, it's also going to realize their fullest bounty."

A rose-beige Mazda nosed up the long drive on the north side of the house. Carl waved toward the car as Kate Klaus, a tall, angular woman, her honey-colored hair skirting her jaws in a bob, began unloading five-gallon plastic buckets of cattails and wild prairie grasses. Earlier in the summer, Kate had offered to arrange flowers for a friend's wedding which was to take place the last weekend in June, but during the month-long drought Kate's usually abundant supply of annuals and perennials had dwindled steadily. Only the purple coneflowers, along with several hybrid daylilies, continued to display robust blooms, so Kate, a native Iowan familiar with indigenous flora, had driven out to the country to forage in the ditches that run between the gravel roads and the corn and soybean fields.

"Kate's the mastermind behind all this. The garden, the house, everything shows her genius. But let's get back to my tomatoes. If you grow tomatoes in cages—and I'm thinking of the large tomatoes—two things happen: one, you delay the arrival of the fruit because they aren't open to the light and able to ripen as quickly as they would like. And two, in this climate and humidity, you get an enormous amount of blight very early on. The moisture just hangs in the cages, which don't allow enough air flow. So from almost the very beginning, I became committed to staking.

"But what I did was try to devise a method that would be both appealing

and productive. And I remember when I first staked tomatoes up and suckered them to just one leader, Kate said they looked like Della Robbias—pendulous, big, plump fruits. But then I discovered that in a very hot summer that method didn't leave enough leaf cover. And without leaf cover, the tomatoes burn before they ripen. So I began experimenting, keeping in mind my goals of beauty and bounty, and I discovered finally that two leaders is just right. That produces handsome tomatoes that weigh anywhere from a half-pound to a pound and a half each."

Carl stepped lightly over the line of bricks and into his garden, its surface blanketed with a layer of golden straw which made the plants appear even lusher and greener than they might have against the backdrop of drought-baked soil. "See this cherry tomato here, the one I call the leader of the band, the one just in front? You'll understand now that I let it grow there not only because it's low-lying, but because I want it to have a lot of room to expand. I want it to be able to go up first, then out gently to the sides, then multiply within itself."

The cherry tomato sprawled at Carl's feet, a mound of wiry branches and tough, hairy leaves in the center, several longer branches vining out toward the sides, the still-green, pea-sized fruit clinging to the stems. Slipping his index fingers into the back pockets of his shorts, Carl studied the plant, smiling as his eyes followed the growth pattern up and out, all of his attention now focused on this one spot in his garden, on this isolated moment of a single plant's development. It was as if for all the digging, all the planning, measuring and planting, all the watering and waiting, this one cherry tomato was reward enough. A minute later, Carl became the English professor once again.

"What I try to do from my experience, my reading, and studying pictures is to understand the ultimate set of conditions necessary to realize the natural beauty of a plant. And throughout the summer I try to take this into account, in respect to plants both individually and collectively. For me, the plant always looks best when it's got the ripe fruit on it. If you go out into a garden in the early morning, say in May, where there's a row of broccoli glistening with dew, it is a stunning sight! And it's not just because the broccoli itself is beautiful, but because the whole plant is beautiful also."

Carl derives the same pleasures from the apricot, pear and apple trees that dot his property. He appreciates them aesthetically for their shapes, the texture of their leaves, and their blossoms, as well as savors their harvest. Later in the afternoon, as we strolled about the yard, he introduced us to each tree as if it were a close friend or a favorite book he had slipped off the library shelf. When he reached the Montmorency cherry, an old variety generally used for pies, he explained that he and Kate had experimented with letting the fruit ripen even longer than was customary and had reaped cherries that were almost as sweet as Bings. "Here, taste this," he invited, picking us a handful, then popping a cherry, its skin musky red and taut, into his own mouth. After exclaiming over the sweetness, he decided to pick us more, and was off toward the house for the ladder and a pail.

While Carl was gone, we explored the more open eastern end of the Klauses' yard: the English yews, the blue spruces, Kate's flower bed laced with exotic varieties of hybrid daylilies—most of them gifts from Fred McDowell, a neighborhood friend and national expert on daylilies; the pear tree; the yellow transparent apple, the base of its trunk already strewn with tiny yellow-green globes; and in the far corner of the yard, three currant bushes, full and rounded, just beginning to set berries.

"Those are purple currants that heretofore you could only find in France," Carl announced, returning with a stepladder balanced over his right shoulder, and a hoe plus an old aluminum pail once used by Kate's grandmother for popping corn gripped in his left hand. When he reached the Montmorency, he gently drew a branch within our reach with the hoe, then mounted the ladder, pinning his hat down on his head with one hand and picking intently with the other. From tree to pail, tree to pail, his hand arced through the air, thumb and forefinger a precision pincers, closing, opening, closing, opening. Carl gathered fruit the way he gardened and the way he spoke, precisely, meticulously, even piously.

Although the heat was not intense that afternoon, the temperature down to 91 after a six-day stretch of 102 and higher, it felt good a half-hour later to leave the open slope of yard and garden, and settle into the metal lawn chairs tucked around the table on the Klauses' back terrace, a *parterre de Versailles* design of limestone squares and concrete rectangles. Shaded by the forty-foot Norway maple, the sunken terrace is a microcosm of the yard, which rises from the east edge of the stone and concrete. Near the table, two hoses, one green and one shiny black, lay in even coils on the ground. At the head of the path leading from the driveway to the terrace, a seedling tray filled with tiny salvia was balanced between two of the metal chairs, and a pair of potted geraniums bloomed in between the legs. Neat clusters of gardening equipment—brooms, kneeling pads, plant food, grass clippers, pruners, seedling trays and several old pairs of huaraches and sneakers—bordered the back door.

Carl slid into one of the lawn chairs, the giant maple leaves rustling above his now-bare head, his hat carefully deposited on top of the pail brimming with warm, ripe cherries. "You know, I started this garden seventeen years ago, a year after we bought the house. It's taken all that time to bring it up to the state you now see it in. And since I was raised a city kid, I've had to pick everything up on my own—from reading, from watching others, and especially from talking to a master gardener named Herman Schroeder. He was a German immigrant who fought for America in World War I, then went into farming. When I knew him, he probably wasn't more than five foot six. He wasn't very long at birth, and he also had an enfeeblement of the hips. Later, age shrank him even more. I used to talk to him for a half-hour or so every night when I walked the dog, and each time I got to know him better. He always had some wisdom. He had one of these metal garden chairs which he set up under an apple tree so that he could see everything. And his yard was just chock-full, with flowers, vegetables and fruit trees planted from one end to the other. What fascinated me about Herman was that here was a man in his eighties tending all of it. And he

couldn't even walk without canes! He couldn't bend at the knees, so he had to garden leaning over a horse. A little wooden sawhorse!"

Carl had discovered a role model, a father figure even, in Herman Schroeder, the diminutive German who poured his physical, emotional and intellectual energies into his vegetables and flowers, inventing new techniques of planting and watering, and always deriving joy from the very act of gardening itself.

"Herman was extraordinary. He actually inspired me. For instance, I realized that if Herman could turn his whole vegetable garden by hand, I could turn mine by hand, too!" From Herman, Carl also learned to know the soil, to understand it, not just by the way it looked, but by the way it felt to the touch. "Herman always spaded his soil in the fall so that it would be open to all the rain during the spring. He explained that if you fine-tilled in September or October, the rain would only pack the soil down. 'But if you till just right,' he used to say, 'come spring, you can touch the soil and it will crumble.'"

From Herman, Carl also learned about water. He learned when planting to irrigate the hole or trench before inserting the seedling, then to cover the watered hole with dry dirt, which would act like a mulch. He also learned to plant his seeds deeper if he anticipated a drought, and to keep his soil cultivated so the intense heat would not bake, then crack, the earth.

And perhaps most important, Carl learned the satisfaction of getting out to the garden at just the right moment after a rain—the second day, or perhaps the third—so he could work the earth at the perfect consistency.

"Herman really was extraordinary. And just about everything he taught me was correct." Carl rocked gently in the chair, flexing and unflexing his hands, the wedding band on his right ring finger tapping against the metal armrest. The chickadee piped up again, and Pip, the Klauses' Welsh terrier, barked back at it. The sweet scent of hyssop wafted toward the patio from the herb bed.

"Oh, and I learned something else from Herman. And that's how to make pea brush. I use that to support my vines instead of chicken wire. What I do is I take twigs left over from pruning, and I put one twig into the earth every three or four inches. Well, I have a double row of peas, and I put a twig on either side of the rows and some in between. And as the peas grow, they form a structure that looks just like a cathedral. It's absolutely beautiful—and sturdy. I've had seventy-mile-an-hour winds hit this brush, and it just stands straight. Yes, I learned this from Herman and you don't see it very often. But the technique goes way back. Once, when I was looking into the books of hours that Kate collects, I came across it."

Carl had mentioned the pea brush to us earlier in the week when we had called to schedule our interview, promising to leave it intact—even though the pea vines had already dried up—so that we could see what the structure looked like. And that afternoon, as soon as we arrived, he had led us to the brush, bending over and delicately fingering several of the sturdy end twigs, which by then had seasoned to a deep golden brown. For Carl, the pea brush was the perfect emblem of his garden: functional, strong, and at the same time beautiful, even beatific. It was also the perfect embodiment of Herman Schroeder.

"So, you see, I learned a lot from Herman, and I followed his methods faithfully until this year. For instance, I never watered in the summers unless it was truly needed. That was what Herman believed in. And I pretty much got away with it because we never had a significant drought. But this year, I began to get very uneasy in May. The temperatures had been unusually high. It was 70 degrees in March. And that was the first sign that we were going to be in trouble. I started watering before the crisis even hit. And during the past month, I've been lugging these two hoses you see down there all around the lot. I start with my red raspberries, then I water the vegetable garden, then on to the corn patch. Next, I get the currant bushes, then Kate's flower bed and the blue spruces. And what I discovered was, as a result of the continuous watering, some things that have never done well before are doing sensationally. For instance, the red raspberries and my asparagus patch actually regenerated!

"So, what I've decided is that Herman's theory probably isn't right for this lot because of all the exposure to the sun. You can see how wide-open the property is, and because of that it's also more exposed to the wind. That's one of the things I've learned to cope with up here on the hill. Most people in the city don't have to pay attention to the wind. But I do a lot with shingles. Whenever I put out a transplant, I stick a shingle in front of it. I call them my sick bays. I just shove the shingle right down into the ground, and leave the seedling behind it for a week to nine days. It takes the plant that long to get used to the harsh prevailing wind up here.

"This doesn't mean that I didn't learn a great deal from Herman. I did. But I have also learned to rely on my own experience, as well as on gardening books. I've a big collection of them in the little bathroom just off the kitchen. In addition, I receive twenty to twenty-five gardening catalogues which I read through every spring. I do that to keep up on what's happening—on what's being bred, what new varieties have come on the market, and which ones have the potential for what I want to achieve. So there's a sense in which I'm always learning and testing. That's how I discovered that the Ace pepper is better here, more productive even in the worst conditions. And there are six different seed companies that carry it."

Carl jumped up and disappeared into the house, his chair bouncing slightly in his wake. The cardinal, quiet for the past half-hour, showered us with song, *what-cheer, what-cheer, what cheer, cheer, cheer*, stopping only when Carl's back door banged and Carl reemerged, his arms loaded with catalogues which he plunked down on the patio table. "Over the winter and during the spring, I read all of these, and I learn something from every one of them. But some are more useful than others." Squinting, he teased several catalogues out from the uneven stack and passed them around, one at a time, the first from the Harris Seed Company in Rochester, New York, one of the most reliable firms, according to Carl, because it prints on the label of every package the percentage of germination. "That way you know immediately how many seeds to plant." Next appeared the Vermont Bean and Seed Company, with a cover photograph featuring a young boy and his grandfather stuffing plastic bags full of tomatoes, peppers, potatoes and squash from the truck stand behind them. Then Stokes, then Thompson and Morgan. And after that, a thin, narrow brochure from Shepherd's Garden Seeds, a new California company specializing in European hybrids unavailable elsewhere.

By reading all the catalogues, Carl tries to keep his garden responsive to the world of hybridizing. For the same reason he subscribes to *Organic Gardening*, *Horticulture*, and *Garden*, paying special attention to their reviews of new seed varieties each year. "Oh, I'm always testing seeds. I look for the best against all other particular varieties of that particular vegetable, the best for our particular region, then area, and then I consider what's best in our particular garden. And believe it or not, it really does work out that way. For instance, I've realized over the past few years that the Supersonic tomato is the one that I should be growing because of the hotness of the sun here."

Carl had recently zeroed in on an optimal variety of cauliflower, too. Named Snow Crown, it was first bred in Japan but was quickly voted an All-American in the United States. It was also through his reading that Carl discovered frost-resistant varieties of all the other vegetables in his spring garden (the Comet broccoli is resistant down to 25 degrees), so that he can now begin transplanting seedlings from his cold frame as early as the first week in April. "And something else. I'm growing two new varieties of onions this year. One is called Mr. Society and it's supposed to be a knockoff of the Vidalia. You know, Vidalia and Maui onions are the sweetest. In fact, they're so sweet you can eat them raw. Well, for many years people claimed these varieties could only be grown in Vidalia, Georgia, or on the island of Maui. But now I have a strain right here in my garden in Iowa City."

A squirrel scampered down from the limb of the maple tree onto the grass, stopping to stare at Carl from its hind legs, its shiny eyes fixed on his back. Then suddenly it scurried off toward the gazebo, an old gardening shed Kate had stripped of shingles and adorned with purple clematis that now winds up the sides on chicken-wire trellises. Through the framework, we could see spades, brooms, hoes and rakes, all gathered in an old crock and propped against one of the corner supports. In another corner, the spouts of three watering cans intersected.

"There's something else I wanted to speak to you about. And that is one of the most important lessons I've gotten out of the experience of gardening: the need to remain flexible and to adapt to a complex set of changing conditions. And I'm talking now about four years of groundhogs and two years of drought. These obstacles have taught me that you can't really tame nature, and yet, ironically, gardening is essentially an attempt to do just that—to subdue, to train, to tame. And you can try to be really canny. You can use your sunshades, dig your trenches, erect your pea brush, but the fact is that there's always something in the set of conditions facing you that will produce an element of frustration, requiring you to bend and reminding you that there are forces much more powerful than you.

"I mentioned the groundhogs a minute ago. They came when the city started to develop Hickory Hill Park behind us. I bought a Havahart trap, but didn't get but one or two groundhogs. Instead I trapped a whole family of possums which I relocated out in the country. And this year in addition to the drought I've been pressing against the grain of a tomato disease. I've always grown my tomatoes in the same place and I've always thought, Well, I'll just grow different varieties. But the reality is, the varieties are not always foolproof."

When Carl led us through his garden earlier in the afternoon, he had pointed out one stricken tomato, its wilted leaves forming a counterpoint to the robust stems and foliage of its companions. Tomato wilt is brought on by either a bacterium or a fungus which causes the leaves to droop severely during the day, then appear to recover in the evening, only to wilt again the next morning. There is no cure for the blight, so most people dig up affected plants and discard them. But Carl refuses. Either too stubborn or too sentimental to concede, he continues to nurse his sick plant, fretting each day when it wilts and rejoicing each evening when it appears to bounce back. But he knows that the stalemate is temporary, that next season the tomatoes will have to be moved.

"As a matter of fact, we just opened up that new stand of corn east of the garden there." Carl raised himself from his seat and craned toward the middle of the lawn where several rows of corn, their leaves slightly curled at the tips, wagged in the early evening breeze. "I used to plant corn on each side of the tomato rows, which meant that I had to shorten the pea rows and cut into the broccoli and cauliflower. Well, of course, I didn't like that cramping, but there was something else that troubled me about having that corn there. The pin oak was encroaching upon it, casting its shade. I wasn't getting good corn on the west end. So this year we spaded up that new plot and put corn and melon there. I used to plant the melon on either side of the cucumbers. In the end, what this new plot enabled me to do was take some of the pressure off my summer garden. And by pressure, I don't mean only pressure for space but, more important, pressure for air. Although you're looking at straw on the ground now, the area will be absolutely covered with green in the fall. You know, the cucumbers will spread, and the tomatoes are just going to flop onto the ground. And actually, what I thought about doing recently was to move the tomatoes up to the new plot and put the corn down in the old garden. I'll leave it there for four or five years until the disease dies off, and then I'll just have an annual or a biannual rotation."

Even though he might be stubborn, reluctant to tamper with his grand scheme, to interfere with the symmetry of color, texture, size and shape he worked so persistently to create, Carl has learned to adapt. He has learned to adapt in his garden, first by experimenting—and being willing to fail—with new varieties of his favorite vegetables, and more recently by rethinking the architecture of his planting. And after two heart attacks and triple-bypass surgery, he has learned to adapt in other areas as well: altering his diet, walking to and from his office each day for exercise, and tempering his natural inclination toward excitement and intense emotion. When Carl speaks about the evolution of his garden, you can't help drawing parallels to his life.

"So, you see I'm talking about what Kate calls the circumstances of an evolving environment. This place is not at all the same as when we first lived here. And I've only just begun to realize how drastically different the circumstances are in my garden from what they were in the beginning. You see that pin oak, that huge pin oak over there?" Carl pointed to the thirty-foot tree, its sharply lobed leaves rising to a triangular crown several yards from his vegetable garden. "We planted that tree in 1971, and here it is seventeen years later, and it's beginning to interfere significantly with my vegetables. And now what I'm beginning to understand is that someday the new corn patch could become my main garden. And this area, which for so long has been the main garden, might be the small one. And that in a way is the epitome of the kind of adjustments a gardener has to live with. So I'm continually relearning a lesson that Kate originally taught me many years ago. Nature is dynamic. It's resilient. It's always changing. You can make small alterations for brief periods, but you have to be willing to accept a lot in gardening. That's really what it is. If you garden you have to accept a lot, and be grateful for whatever you get."

# Chaos among the Cosmos?

## An Interview with Ann and Eric Weir

*Eric and I began gardening together in 1975 in a local park district program, and now have a raised-bed backyard garden with flowers and vegetables in Champaign, Illinois. Eric gardened as a child in east-central Illinois, where his grandfather was a farmer. He is currently working in East Lansing, Michigan, with the Holmes Group, an education consortium. I was inspired to garden by my grandmother, who had a grandmotherly-type garden, with flowers growing everywhere. I am now acquiring editor for literature at the University of Illinois Press, and I recently edited* Prime Number: Seventeen Stories from Illinois Short Fiction.

—Ann Weir, Champaign, Illinois

It was the hottest day of a summer plagued by heat waves and drought. All week temperatures had hovered around 105 degrees, and during the ride from Iowa to Illinois the sky, a gray tent of stagnant air, had pushed the humidity back down onto the asphalt of Interstate 80 and the surrounding farmlands, where everything—corn, barns, soil, ditch grass—looked brown. In town, sidewalks were empty, traffic thin, the hum of cicadas and air conditioners loud.

But even at four o'clock that afternoon, in full bleached orange sun, with absolutely no breeze, Ann and Eric Weir's garden looked cool, an oasis of deep green splotched with yellows, oranges and reds. Along the border closest to the house, dense clumps of marigolds squatted, bursting with blossoms. Tomatoes and dill, broccoli, squash and beans flourished behind the flowers. And interspersed with the vegetables, red salvia, nasturtiums and more marigolds grew in spikes, vines and clusters. Contrasting with the color, a mulch of straw, crisp and clean, protected the soil, sparser between the rows and mounded near the plants. At the far end of the plot, Eric, his T-shirt dark with sweat, bent over a dandelion. A pile of discarded weeds rose beside him.

"Don't take too long, Eric, or we'll have to start without you." Ann leaned over the railing of the small deck built onto the dining room of their frame house, her sundress billowing out from her legs. She was tall, angular, her broad shoulders accented by the straps of the red-and-white sleeveless bodice that lay flat against her chest. Her cap of wavy brown hair was cropped close at the neck.

Eric lifted his head. "I'm going to be awhile. I want to get rid of this creeping charlie. It's taking over. And then I have to pinch back the broccoli."

"Eric's real fussy about the garden. He likes the rows to be cut down with razor-sharp edges and everything to be picked on schedule. I think that streak is inherited from his grandfather. And he really tends to get carried away with this weeding, especially now that he works up in East Lansing. When he comes home on weekends, he's worse than ever. I can't garden that way. I like to have dill just growing up in the middle of everything. And cosmos all over the place."

Although they agree on a lot of things, like the impeccably refinished oak antiques they have furnished their home with, the Weirs have differing philosophies on gardening. And they are vocal about them. Eric, who was

raised in a strict German family, grew up not far from Champaign, Illinois, on a farm where the work ethic kept the rows straight and the children picking beans. And although Ann also grew up in the Midwest, her family lived in town, where the gardens were more casual and decorative, cultivated for variety, primarily to please the eye. An advocate of order and purpose, Eric becomes serious and philosophical when he talks about gardening, reflecting as much on spirit as technique. Ann remains more concrete and personal, and prefers to stick close to her own expertise and experience.

"I guess we'll have to start without Eric. He'd just disagree with what I say, anyway. He can give his side later. I know one of the things he'll tell you is that I don't let him plant enough. But, for Pete's sake, we still have a whole freezer full of vegetables from last year's garden. I mean, two people can only eat so much. And he'll also probably say that he wants to plant in triangles, more in beds than in rows. And that I have too many flowers. He complains that my salvia, cosmos and marigolds are taking up too much room."

Ann dumped a tray of ice into a jar of tea, grabbed a stack of plastic tumblers off a kitchen shelf and led us across the street to the neighborhood park, which she and Eric had decided would be cooler than their house. The Weirs have no air conditioning, only a 1930s oscillating pole fan. And with the heat built up all day inside, the fan, stationed in the doorway between kitchen and dining room, chugged to cut through the late afternoon sultriness.

"When we started our first garden, we were living in our apartment, and I guess I just saw something in the paper about how the Urbana Park District was creating the Meadowbrook Program out there on Windsor Road. They had just plowed it up and staked it. And they said Saturday morning, at such and such a time, they were having this meeting. I said to myself, Well, that might be nice. So, Eric and I went over and signed up for a plot."

Ann unfolded slung canvas lawn chairs at the edge of the park under a canopy of sycamores and elms, and plopped down the jar of iced tea. The sun glinted off her dark glasses as she leaned back, crossed one long leg and draped her dress over her knee. Her foot began to jiggle immediately. Behind her on the other side of the park, the slide and swing set stood empty.

"Until Meadowbrook, I had never really gardened, although my parents had a garden during World War II, before I was born. But then they never had much of one after that. I remember my father's mother had a garden when I was little—sort of a grandmotherly type of plot, with stuff all over the place, flowers and everything. But Eric was the expert. His maternal grandfather was a farmer. And when Eric was little, his family had big gardens and he had to help. Eric's father would tell the kids, 'Today before you play, you have to pick one row of beans, or two bushelbaskets of beets.' Then later, he'd go check the rows, and if the kids hadn't gotten all the beans, they had to go back over the row again.

"Because he grew up on a farm, when we started our garden, Eric knew something about raising vegetables—as he kept telling me. And I didn't know anything. So I thought, OK. I'll go and take the organic gardening course at Parkland Junior College. There, I learned about starting little seedlings in peat pots and soil testing and all that stuff. But that was the only kind of study I ever did."

Their first year at the community gardens, Ann and Eric were lucky. The weather remained mild with periodic thunderstorms, and in late August they picked perfect tomatoes from vines sprawling over the flat, bare earth. "I mean, the tomatoes didn't get fusarium wilt or anything. And we kept saying to ourselves, Hey, this is OK!" The next year, the Weirs signed up for two plots, expanding their garden to include corn and squash. "Of course, we never were as lucky as that first year. When you garden, one year like that is about all you get out of I don't know how many." Then Ann and Eric bought a house in Champaign, on the other side of town, and began gardening at home—although that season they continued to raise corn and squash, which require space but little maintenance, in the community garden, gathering all their implements and shuttling over to Meadowbrook every few weeks to tend the plot.

"And we could have kept up the community garden forever, just growing squash and corn and things that did not require a lot of upkeep, but pretty much got ripe all at one time. But it was an interactive situation at Meadowbrook. The whole point was to go out and see what everybody else was doing. And if you only plant and then go back every few weeks just to weed and pick, you're not participating in the nature of the program the way the park district set it up. At least, I don't think you are. So, we quit doing that. And, besides, we have more room in the backyard than we need."

An acquiring editor for literature at the University of Illinois Press, Ann is a hawkish reader who tones and corrects manuscripts to bring them as close to perfection as possible. But her speech is freer than her blue pencil, full of colloquialisms and vagaries as well as erudition. And her voice is labile, authoritative one minute and singsong the next.

"Of course, here, Eric and I have our disagreements. Raspberries are just about my favorite thing in the world. I just love them. But Eric doesn't like ours where they are. He keeps insisting we move them from along the driveway to the raised beds in the back. But there are already single-crop raspberries and blackberries along the lot line in the backyard, and I've heard you're not supposed to grow one kind of berry less than a certain distance from another kind—or you really start getting disease. And we've already had a problem with our raspberries. For the first few years we lived here, they did fine. Then in 1981, I noticed that this one area seemed sort of dead. And I thought, What happened to these guys?

"So I dug one up and took it out to the extension place, and the man there said it had . . . I think it was anthracnose. Our sycamore tree sometimes gets that in the spring. The leaves are little, and they all just fall off and the tree has to start all over. The man at the extension said, 'Oh, yeah, same kind of thing. They're all going to die and you can't grow raspberries

within a hundred yards of there in the future.' And I said to myself, Well, that kind of terminates the raspberry operation.

"But I didn't give up right away. I thought, Maybe he's wrong. At that time, my father had been getting the newsletter of the American Fruit Explorers, which is called *Pomona*. I wrote to the guy for the bramble division and explained that the raspberries were along the driveway and got full afternoon sun, and they had anthracnose. Then I asked him, 'What should I do short of digging them up and planting petunias there?' He advised weeding out all the diseased canes, then cutting them totally back in the fall. Because the raspberries were everbearing, I hated to do that. But I did. And it worked! And now every time Eric says, 'Ann, I'm going to move the raspberries,' I tell him, No."

Ann laughed, a nervous giggle. Against the deep green of the canvas behind her, her flesh looked white, the veins visible through the transparent skin on her arms. Her tent dress, which rose and fell with each breath, collapsed onto her lap as she craned toward the house and scanned the yard for Eric, who hadn't yet appeared.

"Eric also thinks my rabbit cages are ridiculous. When we were out at Meadowbrook, the rabbits weren't a problem. With all the other gardens, there was just too much for them to eat. And actually, we didn't have a big problem here until about three or four years ago. Eric says we must've moved in on the 'up cycle.' And I think they have to be ready for the 'crash and die off' phase by now. Every year I keep saying to myself, There can't be any more rabbits.

"But the next year there are always more. And they make gardening so much work. You know, instead of just going and putting out these little broccoli plants, either you've got to make these little cages out of chicken wire, or you've got to fence the entire area. Well, Eric laughs at my cages, but I tell him, 'Rabbits won't eat pepper. They won't eat squash. They won't eat tomatoes. They won't eat basil. So seventy-five percent of what we plant, they're not going to bother.'"

To protect their cool-weather crops, Ann constructs cages of chicken wire, a foot high and eighteen inches long, weaving the ends together to form cylinders. Then she anchors the cages into the ground with coat hangers, and plants the seedlings inside. By the time the leaves are big enough to burst the confines of the wire, they're tough. "And the rabbits would rather look for something else."

Eric finally arrived, his hair slicked back from a shower, and slipped into the empty chair beside Ann. Beads of moisture still clung to the tip of his sharp nose. With his middle finger, he poked his wire-rimmed glasses up toward his forehead, then patted his brow with a white handkerchief folded into quadrants, tucking it behind his knee when he was finished. Eric's face was lean, cheeks hollow, his legs and body disciplined and tight, honed by years of triathlon training, beginning with jogging in 1973, then adding cycling and, more recently, swimming. He had changed clothing after gardening, and his cotton shorts and shirt fell loosely over his trim torso.

"I was just talking about our disagreements. I told them how you hate my little clumps."

"I don't hate clumps."

"Are you kidding?"

"I'm telling you, I don't hate clumps."

"But stuff in the aisles drives you insane."

"You mean like flowers going to seed and then growing back up so you can't get down the rows?"

Ann poured Eric some iced tea, careful to allow only one cube to drop into his glass. "Because we disagree a lot, we've learned to do different things in the garden. I figure out what we're going to grow, order the seeds and start and plant them. And Eric usually digs, helps with the mulch, weeds and picks. And he pounds in the tomato cages. Then I freeze everything."

"Well, I'd like to have more say about what we're going to plant."

"I already told them you'd like to plant more, especially Chinese vegetables."

"Did you tell them about the raised beds?"

"Raised beds were Eric's idea. But I don't think they work out very well around here. They're supposed to allow you to get started gardening earlier in the spring. You know, you raise the soil above ground level and it warms up and dries out quicker. But then, at least the way it's been around here the last few years, pretty soon you have to start watering and mulching. And I'm not sure it's worth all the work. This spring, it rained so little that mulching the raised beds was like mulching a sandbox."

"That's because I was away and the beds weren't kept up well enough. And that gets me kind of mad because I worked so hard digging them in the first place. What I really should have done was establish a wooden barrier around each bed and build up the soil in that. Instead, I did it the hard way, and shoveled out one whole layer, tossed that to the side, then excavated a second layer, filling in the bed with the soil from the first. And if the excavating wasn't bad enough, getting the beds fairly level turned out to be almost as tough a job."

"Poor Eric!"

"Ann never wanted raised beds in the first place. I'd talked them up from the time we began gardening, but with no success. When we moved into this house, the people had a lawn on one side of the yard, and a garden on the other. Ann and I doubled that, with a grass strip in between. But we had our rows going east and west, which is not the way they should go because that cuts down on a lot of light. So, I kept saying, 'Ann, we should just take out that strip in the middle, turn these rows around, and orient the garden to the north and south. And we can make raised beds while we're at it.'

"But Ann is a person who gets on a rail and just goes. She said, 'No,' she wasn't going to hear anything about it. So one spring I guess I kind of hit her with a tank. I got up early while she was still in bed, and I just started. Our bedroom is in the back of the house, and a few hours later when Ann rolled the shades up and saw what I had done, she was irate. But that's the way we make changes in our lives."

A woman in a halter top wheeled a baby stroller down the sidewalk by the park. A toddler pumped along on a tricycle behind her, a Tonka truck attached to the seat post with a string, scraping over the cement. Across the park two men began a game of tennis. Their sneakers scuffed as the ball, a chartreuse blur, streaked over the net and bounced outside the service line. "Fifteen-love."

Ann smoothed her skirt over her knee. "I told them how you want the garden to be neat, and that any deviation seems horrendous to you. You know, you keep complaining that I have flowers all over the place."

"I think you've got me wrong. I'm not for geometry. And I hate English gardens. They're too intricate. But I want my garden to be aesthetic. And when things just crop up out of nowhere . . . "

"But I think that's kind of neat. I like the way the dill comes up all over the place, or coriander, or feverfew."

"It's fine if *some* things just grow. But I don't like to let *everything* just grow. You have to work toward a pattern. I don't want my garden to be wild. I want to work with it. I want to shape it without controlling it. You know, I would never go so far as to trim my vegetables so that they have the right form. But I think a new garden with all its straight rows is so beautiful."

The Weirs also disagree about leaf mulch. In the fall, Ann rakes all the leaves—maples, sycamores, locusts—and spreads them over the garden soil. Then she places tomato cages around the edge to keep most of the mulch from blowing off. "I know tomato cages aren't ideal, but they do keep the leaves there for awhile. And then the soil doesn't have to go through so much freezing and thawing, freezing and thawing."

"I don't see much point in doing that. Freezing and thawing is normal. It can't be bad for the earth. Of course, what Ann does would be all right if she let the leaves deteriorate first. Or, at least, shredded them. But now with her method they just get matted."

"Well, at least it keeps the soil from packing down hard. And the locust leaves decompose."

"Instead of the leaf mulch, I've toyed with the idea of putting in a cover crop like rye or buckwheat. I understand that if you don't let it get established like a lawn, it keeps the weeds down and helps loosen the soil."

"But that would never work around here. Like this spring, one day it was cold, and the next day it was hot. There wasn't any time in between. Then other seasons, it rains or stays cold, and you're lucky if you have one day when you can get out in the garden and work before it rains again. Well, if that one day is when you're digging up buckwheat, you're really out of luck."

"Ann and I have all sorts of little disagreements about gardening. But here's the main difference between us. Ann knows a lot about gardening now, and a lot of it she has learned recently. But most of it she has gotten from books. And she can cite chapter and verse about why, and so forth. But for me, I just *do* it. The garden's just there."

"Eric's the intuitive gardener."

"I mean I'm interested in learning and trying new things. But a lot of what I know, I've grown up with. And if I had more time, if I didn't have this job which took me away so much, I would experiment and garden more like Edward Diobbi. His *Italian Family Cookbook* makes wonderful

reading. Diobbi gardened. He fished. And he put up food. And he tells stories in his book. In one of my favorites, he tells about a visit to Sicily when his eighty-year-old grandfather drank him under the table."

It was five o'clock, the temperature and humidity holding steady. The sycamore leaves, prematurely brown from the drought, hung motionless above our heads. The cicadas thrummed like a pulse. A family trio, two older brothers and a younger girl yelling "Hey, you guys, wait for me," ran between us toward the swings as they cut the corner on the park. The tennis match moved into the second set. And despite the persistent heat, the stale air, the conversation shifted keys.

"What I remember best from growing up was when I was ten or eleven, summertimes like this, just for fun going out into the garden." Eric rubbed his hand back and forth over his sandaled foot, beginning near his toes, then following the curve of his instep. "We had a big plot and a big culti-vator. And I would run that thing up and down the rows. I'd create patterns in the soil. Of course, part of what I was doing was pretending I was my grandfather on his tractor."

"I think Eric would like the garden to become a larger part of our life than it is. He'd like to plant and preserve even more than we do now. And I know that he would like to keep building up the soil in the beds. When we first moved here he made a compost bin, and then one fall he hauled in these loads of manure and put it all over the garden. But for composting you really need a shredder, and in order to have the right kind of shredder—I mean one that doesn't jam up from one marigold—you need to pay nine hundred dollars.

"There are some things we agree on, though. Like we don't grow zucchini anymore. Because of the squash bugs, it's just too difficult. You know, you put the seeds in, the plants begin to thrive, and then they're killed, just like that. Either that, or they're not killed, and then you're worse off.

"Once when we still had zucchini, we gave some to a friend. And in the morning, when she came down to her kitchen, the zucchini had emulsified into this blob of goo all over her counter. But the real problem with zucchini is when you get them, it's right when the beans and all sorts of other vegetables are ripe. And you are always figuring, With all this zucchini, we'd better eat some of it tonight. And so you end up eating this stupid zucchini fresh and freezing all the good stuff. Finally I thought, I keep giving all these people zucchini. I'll just let someone give me some once in awhile. So we quit growing it. And do you know what? No one has ever given us *one* zucchini!"

"We also don't try to grow cantaloupes anymore. Did Ann tell you about that? She wanted to grow cantaloupe. And I kept telling her, 'You can't grow it around here. They need sandy, well-drained soil.' But Ann insisted. So she planted two rows. And the fruit developed all right. But as soon as it matured, it rotted. We tried everything. We put straw under the fruit, cardboard and newspapers to protect them. With all that work, we finally got one cantaloupe out of the two rows. But I must admit, it was good, really good."

"At least I knew more about gardening than Beldon Keal." Ann giggled. "Poor Beldon. He was a political science professor and gardened out at Meadowbrook when we were there."

"Oh, yes, Beldon was trying to be the good New Age person, growing his own food and going back to nature. He was the consummate intellectual."

"So he planted all these things, and when they started growing, he asked us, 'Could you come over to my plot for a moment, because I don't know what any of this stuff is.' "

"Of course," Eric said, "I appreciated what Beldon was doing. I think a family our size could certainly subsist on a garden. I know we could. And

I had thought many times that if I didn't finish my dissertation, or a job didn't work out for me, my profession would be at home, cooking and gardening.

"For instance, I hadn't planned to be working out in the garden this afternoon when you came. I'd gone out to do a little bit of shopping, and when I came back, you weren't here yet. So I mowed the yard, and while I was mowing, I noticed these weeds in the garden and I started pulling. We'd watered, and it's real hot, so the weeds came up easily. And there's something about that, some pleasure in being able to get the whole weed to come clean out of the soil. And in getting your garden tidied up. If you're able to get a big spreading patch of crab grass out without pieces breaking off, it just feels good.

"You know, once you've gotten the garden established, you can come home from work, and go out and see what's there, just sort of poke around and pull things up and pinch things back. If a squash plant's getting out of its territory, you flip it back. Or, you go through the tomatoes and break off the suckers. And watering. Just standing and watering. I enjoy doing that. It's almost a form of meditation."

We could imagine Eric, white frame house behind him, at the edge of his lawn where the straw met the grass in a clean line, directing the stream of water from the hose, first to the base of the tomatoes, going down the rows, letting the water pool, then drain, then pool again, then moving to the beans, his thumb over the nozzle, the water spraying on the pods, drizzling down the leaves and onto the golden mulch below.

"And also," Ann said, "gardening makes you more conscious of the way things are. I'm aware of this especially because there are so many students around here. And they always want it to be sunny, no clouds, about 84 degrees. If every day is like that, they think it's perfectly fine. You can have a summer like this one where the grass is totally shriveled up, and they just love it. And then there's the people who are off in their air-conditioned houses, and pay Tru Green to come and defoliate everything so that they can have their comforts. Well, that's denying nature.

"You know, I'll say, 'I wish it would rain. I wish it would rain.' And people will respond, 'Oh, I don't want it to rain. I want to go to the lake tomorrow.' When they say that, I think, Well, too bad.

"Also, having a garden, you notice more. Like you notice *if* it's going to

rain. And your opinion of the weather is based on your garden, not on your own convenience. And then there's the seasonal aspect of things. In the spring, you plant all these vegetables and flowers, and the rows are so far apart that your garden looks pathetic. You have this big area of dirt, and these tiny marigolds about two inches tall. And then, by the beginning of June, there's just these nice teenage-type marigolds. Then they all get real big and shoot out all over the place. And then in the fall, they all go *chtttt* one day and die. And that's the way things are. A lot of people don't notice any of that. They miss making connections between themselves and nature."

Eric ran his index finger along his sandal strap. "I think in addition to noticing more and being more aware of things, like the seasons and plants growing and changing, with working in a garden, especially when you do it organically, there's a kind of challenge in trying to grow food without chemicals. You end up working with the plants, becoming part of the garden and being shaped by it. Instead of trying to control, instead of trying to mangle and trying to do things your way, you learn how the garden can go, and you go with it. You end up feeling a kind of connectedness with something bigger."

It was dinnertime now, the park and street deserted, the intense humidity slowing down all movement and muffling sound. Eric reached for the handkerchief under his thigh to dab at the perspiration on his forehead. With her index finger, Ann skimmed the condensation off her glass of tea.

"You know," Eric continued, "this may sound like a silly example, but broccoli is a vegetable I've learned to work with. I like broccoli and I like growing it. Those first heads form and you cut that, and it's heavy and, well, it's beautiful. And then if you let the plant alone, it will put out a lot of little shoots. There'll be so many florets that you can stand for hours at one plant picking.

"So what I do now is, I pick the first head, then go around the plant and cut off all the little buds until I reach the top. There, I leave two to four buds. And from those, you'll get a second crop of heads. And you can cut those buds off again, and continue like that all summer long.

"When I was younger, I wanted to be a farmer. I worked for a landscape contractor in Pennsylvania and seriously considered going back to school in horticulture. We often had to dig up large shrubs and trees from my boss's nursery. Once, we were excavating a huge oak tree, and the ground under it was basically clay and shale. There was almost no topsoil. I told the people I was working with, 'There are hundreds and hundreds and thousands of acres out in the Midwest. You can drive for miles and you can run a spade into the ground and there are no rocks.'"

Ann and Eric are attached to the land. And despite their disagreements and disputes, gardening creates a sense of well-being, a vein of harmony, in their lives. Though they may argue over raised beds or cultivated rows, leaf mulch or winter wheat, after fifteen years of working the soil as a couple they have woven a history for themselves, one large enough in time and space to incorporate both contradiction and convergence—from Eric's childhood fantasies on the family cultivator and Ann's grandmother's garden with its hint of chaos, to their first perfect Meadowbrook tomatoes in 1975. And whatever transformations their circumstances undergo—Ann's promotion at the press, even Eric's new job, which takes him to East Lansing each week—their backyard plot remains central to their lives, visible from almost every room in their house—downstairs through the sliding glass doors off the combination living/dining room, as well as through the bay above the kitchen sink, and upstairs from the double windows in the bedroom where each morning they roll up the shades and look out.

"And you know, Eric, we forgot to tell them about the soup, the chicken won ton soup. We were thinking about this recently when we were having dinner in this little Korean restaurant downtown. Whenever we eat there, we remember another time. It was the second year we had a garden at Meadowbrook, the year we had two plots. And we went out there in the fall to clean out all this stuff. It was in November and it was overcast and gloomy when we went out. By the time we got there, it was misting."

"Yes, we wanted to clean off the garden," Eric chimed in. "And there was a big pile of manure they'd hauled from a farm nearby. And out at Meadowbrook, you'd get a plot, and you were responsible for maintaining the whole thing. You'd have to clear it off and spade it. That day we wanted to clean up both plots and put a cover of manure on. All in one day."

"So we got out there," Ann said, "and it was pretty cold and overcast and misty. Then it started raining. But we stayed and dragged away the debris. And Eric was hauling over all this manure. I don't know how long it took. We must've been out there for hours in the rain. We came back home finally. We were so cold. We took showers and went down to the little Korean restaurant, and had these big bowls of chicken won ton soup. And that was about the best soup we ever had."

# A Loaf of Bread
# and a Flower

An Interview with

Larry and Marian Fischer

*I grew up in the small town of Manning, Iowa, and graduated
from Iowa State University in 1967 with a B.S. degree in engineering. Shortly before graduating, Marian and I were married—and after graduation moved to Saint Charles, Illinois.
After two years of commuting to Automatic Electric in North-
lake, I decided that city living wasn't for me—and we moved to
the small southern Minnesota town of Waseca where I accepted
an engineering position with the Johnson Company. After one
year in town, we purchased an old run-down ten-acre farm site
and have been repairing, rebuilding and remodeling (and everything else one does on a hobby farm) ever since—including
raising children—two boys: Andrew, ten, and Alan, eight.*

*My interest in gardening goes back to when I was four or five
years old, and my mother taught me how little seeds grow into
plants. My interest was nurtured by a neighbor, F. J. ("Bud")
McMahon, who ran the feed and seed store in our little town. I*

planted my first garden when I was six and have had a garden every year since.

—Larry Fischer, Waseca, Minnesota


Born the oldest of seven children, I grew up on a northeast Iowa dairy farm near Readlyn. As the oldest, I spent countless hours in the fields, where I developed a deep appreciation for the quiet and beauty of nature.

I also attended Iowa State University, and after marrying Larry, finished my B.S. degree in food science at Northern Illinois University in De Kalb. After moving to Waseca, I worked for four years as a lab technician for General Foods—and then returned to college—this time to Mankato State University, where I received my M.B.A. Since then I have been playing "mother" and "gardener" and "homemaker" and "construction worker" and whatever else my husband needs—and loving every minute of it.

Although my dear old German grandparents were gardeners, my mother was too busy to garden. It was my husband who rekindled my childhood love for flowers and soils and nature.

—Marian Buhr Fischer, Waseca, Minnesota

"Our gardens are the reason we have these chickens in the first place. Chicken manure is the highest in nitrogen of all the fertilizers. Plus we incorporate it with the straw that comes out of the roosts." Larry Fischer knelt on the floor of his chicken coop. Above his head, a dozen Rhode Island Red hens hovered over their nests, while at his feet, eight goslings, their down yellowish green, bills translucent, waddled for cover under the brooder. A red building with fresh white trim, the coop abuts the mounded rows of Larry and Marian Fischer's vegetable garden, which overlooks their seven-acre farm atop a rise in southern Minnesota, a sweep of land the Fischers have planted from barn to road with rose gardens, flower beds, shade trees and prairie grasses.

"The gardens and Aunt Lilly," Marian said, reaching into one of the nests for a brown-and-white speckled egg. "Larry's Aunt Lilly comes to visit every few months, and stays from two to three weeks. And she always takes care of the chickens. In the middle of the winter, she'll put on my snowsuit and boots, and there she is, eighty-some years old, trudging over to the coop. I always accuse her of talking to the hens."

If you ask Larry and Marian Fischer, gardening is the reason for the whirl of activity, the chronic industry, in a family life that includes chicken raising, canning, composting, tree trimming, barn building and house restoring. The Fischers bought their acreage outside of Waseca, Minnesota, where Larry is an electronics engineer, with the desire to renew and cultivate its farm and woodlands. And for the past fourteen years they have worked steadily, transforming a neglected collection of buildings and stagnant acres into a family homestead. In the process, they have created a botanical showcase, written up in *Minnesota Horticulture* and visited each summer by a stream of local and imported garden lovers. But underlying all the Fischers' projects, the intricately laid-out beds and flowing fountains, the cement-block tunnel connecting kitchen and fruit cellar, the A-frame cucumber trellises and forty varieties of bearded iris, is the couple's compulsion to sustain the past within the present, while they keep the family—grandparents, sisters, brothers, aunts, uncles, and cousins—together.

For the Fischers garden seasons, ornaments, vegetables and flowers provoke a flood of associations. The cedar benches at the mouth of the woods recall Marian's brother, who crafted them over several summers. Larry associates kale with his German grandmother, the spring rows of carrots with

his mother. And jam making, canning and chicken slaughtering are excuses for family reunions.

"We can every year at my mother's," Marian said. "Not because it's economically feasible, but because it's fun for the grandchildren. All the aunts and cousins get together around a huge old table in the basement, each with our own knife, and cut up vegetables and meat, preparing them for the jars, then the pressure cooker. Larry and I save the tallow from our chickens because my grandmother always insisted that there be fat on top to help seal the jar tight.

"And then in the fall, we have our annual chicken slaughter here. All our hens are broilers, and we like to butcher those ourselves. My mother and sisters and their kids always come up to help. And once again, the whole family works together. Larry gets up early in the morning and starts the fire. We have a big copper boiler we set up over an open flame. I go into the chicken house and catch the birds, then I hand them out the door to my little sister Trina, who takes them by the foot over to my mother, who stands there with a butcher knife, cuts off their heads, then throws their bodies over to Larry. He dips the chickens in the boiler and scalds them."

Both Larry and Marian thrive on hard work. By the time he was twelve, Larry had his own small business mowing lawns for eleven different neighbors in his hometown of Manning, Iowa. On Saturdays he would race from one yard to the next, working so intently that once he ran the mower over his work boot, slicing off his big toe. The lawns finished, he would work along with some of these neighbors in their gardens. In addition, Larry maintained a plot of his own. "I probably started when I was in second or third grade, in a space behind the garage three feet wide and five feet long, with a couple of rows of lettuce, carrots and beets. Mom would give me a few seeds, or I'd go downtown and for ten cents get more seeds than you could ever imagine. I always had flowers, too."

Inside the Fischers' screened-in front porch with its vista of hackberries, silver maples, walnuts and Kentucky coffee trees trailing down to a bank of cottonwoods along the creek, Larry set down a tray of soda and ice on the rattan table. Over six feet tall, he folded himself up on the love seat next to Marian, hugging his knees, his legs drawn up to his chest, bare heels digging into the wicker. His cotton safari shorts fell away from his thighs. It was only May, but Larry was already deeply tanned, the crown of his close-cropped sandy hair bleached a shade lighter, his muscles articulated from the spring gardening he and Marian had begun in March.

For Marian, working outdoors is a birthright, the eight months every year she spends tending and cultivating the Fischers' grounds the legacy of a farm girl intimate with the rituals of raising corn or castrating hogs. "Growing up on a farm, I'm an outdoors person. I was used to herding cows and going down to the woods and riding horses. For me, being outside is essential. I don't care if it's in the field, or the garden, on the lawn or in the woods."

Marian does not cut the figure of a homesteader. Long-legged and lithe, with shoulder-length blond hair drawn up in a ponytail, she moves more like a dancer than a farmer. Her voice is wispy, girlish, the words tumbling out in phrases, each syllable precisely enunciated. Yet Marian began working with her father on the farm before she was even tall enough to reach the clutch pedal on the tractor.

"Actually I grew up in kind of a neat environment. While I was living at home, no one told me you can't do this or that because you are a woman. I remember when I started driving the John Deere I was only six. My father had already mowed the hay and it was in little windrows around five feet wide. And he needed it side-raked. So, he made one trial round, put the tractor in gear, and sent me on my way. He returned just when I had finished and we went back to the house together. And later, when I was sixteen, my father bought a load of hay from a farmer south of Des Moines, and he had me drive the semi six hours round trip from Readlyn to pick it up.

"But that was all good practice for the driving I do around here. About four times a year, I take our pickup over to the sawmill in Norseland for sawdust and wood chips. After the truck's loaded, I take a tarp and wrap it around the bed like a baby's diaper, and then when I get home, I shovel everything out."

Marian and Larry spread the wood chips for mulch around their trees and shrubs, a necessity in their windswept location where forty-five-mile-an-hour gusts are common. The sawdust, they smooth along the paths in their vegetable garden to keep both moisture in and mud out. Like plush carpeting, the sawdust paths muffle all friction and sound, and combine with the hay mulch layered on top of the raised beds to give the vegetable garden the appearance of a Van Gogh landscape.

Initially, the Fischers gardened in flat beds without mulch and sawdust, but because their soil was heavy clay loam, they had trouble with drainage. "One year we had only two inches of edible flesh on our carrots." Larry pointed to the second joint of his index finger. "Everything below that had rotted. The next year we started gardening with raised beds and mulch. The raised beds dry out early in the spring and we are able to get our crops in faster."

Larry and Marian mulch their mounds with grass hay, or marsh hay baled from the old swamps and sloughs that dot Minnesota. If they can't obtain wild hay, they use alfalfa hay rather than oat straw, which has too many residual seeds.

"If we used straw, all spring we'd be on our hands and knees pulling weeds," Larry said. "So we mulch with hay, and in October when it's turned golden yellow, we dig the hay under with the chicken manure. In the winter, we like to look out our upstairs window at the mounds below and watch the way the snow drifts up against them, the way they're almost backlit by a full moon. Then in March the thaw gradually uncovers this rich black dirt."

Beautiful as well as functional, the Fischers' raised beds combine the two passions of Larry and Marian's life. Their gardening techniques have been selected to promote the health and productivity of the plants, but these methods also conform to the couple's aesthetic, which appeals to the eye as well as to a sense of order. The Fischers' gardens are laid out in geometric designs, the roses patterned in triangles, the flower beds in staggered rows, the vegetable plot in a series of elongated, identically contoured mounds. And until the Fischers' two sons, Alan and Andrew, now eight and ten, were born, the vegetable garden was organized into quadrants.

"We used to measure the plot out on paper first. Then each spring we'd set up the stakes, run strings between them and plant within the quadrants. But with the babies around, we stopped gardening that way. I believe in spending time with my children," Marian said. Behind her, the leaves on the silver maple glinted as the wind rose, setting off the chimes hanging from the soffits of the porch. Marian's bangs fluttered up from her forehead and a Baltimore oriole whistled from the limb of a cottonwood.

The Fischers have not always gardened with such scale and elegance. Larry carved out their first plot behind their small apartment in Ames, Iowa, while they were still students.

"We were married in late May, too late to till a plot. We were trying to move into this cruddy old apartment. The cupboards were awful. But even before we had the kitchen cleaned up, Larry was out there. He was just sure we needed a garden."

Larry edged toward Marian and stroked her knee. "We even had a garden in a duplex outside of Chicago. The people upstairs who owned the building didn't do any gardening, so we took care of all the fruit trees for them."

"Something we did there still bothers me," Marian said. "We moved out of that place in August or September, and we had been watching the pear trees. They were just loaded that year. And pears have to be picked before they're ripe. So, the morning we were leaving—the moving truck had already gone—we got up and picked all the pears off the trees and stuffed them into an old pillowcase. Then we loaded them into our little '61 Falcon and went off to my mother's and canned pears the next week."

The Fischers' first flower garden on the Waseca acreage was a bed of thirty tulips, a gift from Bud McMahon, one of Larry's neighbors in Manning, Iowa. Democratic party organizer, public school superintendent and owner of McMahon Feed and Seed on Main Street, Bud was a lover of birds and flowers. He was also a pied piper. Every night with his wife, Elsie, a stash of caramel candies in his pocket, he led nature walks through town, down First Street, up Second past the Lutheran and Methodist churches, heading north, a trail of children growing behind them.

"Gosh, Bud was the type of fellow you could sit on the front porch with, and he'd always tell some story. And all the kids would have questions for him about plants, flowers, birds and trees. I wasn't always sure if he was telling me the truth or ad-libbing, but Bud always had an answer."

McMahon Feed and Seed, the gardening center of Manning, was a cramped space wedged between the furniture store and the dairy, its ten-foot-high shelves stacked with trowels, gloves, asparagus and horseradish roots, daffodil and crocus bulbs. The wooden floor, swept with red sawdust, was mounded with feed sacks, fertilizers and cans of pesticide. Customers would scoop bulk seeds from bins and interrupt the daily pinochle game with questions about blood meal and cabbage transplants.

"We'd go down there and say, 'Bud, what type of radish are you going to plant this year?' Well, whatever Bud had ordered was obviously the best.

In those days, nobody in Manning ever started seedlings at home. Bud had so many in flats and the plants were only ten cents apiece.

"Bud was a big influence on me. In fact, when I was in sixth grade, at his urging I made a flower arrangement and entered it in the junior division of the garden club flower show. The arrangement was in a bunny vase which I still have and I won first place. Later, Bud moved from Manning to a farm near Independence, Iowa, not far from where Marian grew up. So, until he died, when we'd go see Marian's mother, we'd visit Bud, too. And every time we saw him, he'd take us for another walk down to the Wapsi-pinicon River near his house. There was a little bridge over the water, and we'd stand there while he pointed out the bloodroot and spring beauties, the wild roses. And along the road on the way back he'd identify bird calls. There'd be red-winged blackbirds, goldfinches and wrens. He'd learned them all off a record he'd bought from Cornell University."

While Larry had been raised in town in a garden-intensive neighbor-hood, Marian grew up on a dairy farm where her father worked the corn and soybean fields alone and her mother rose at five each morning to milk the Guernseys. Their workdays were ten hours long. For Marian's parents, the cows, pastures and fields were income, not pleasure. Although Marian's mother would occasionally cultivate a vegetable garden, she never planted flowers.

"My grandpa was German and very practical and my mother was just like him. She always said, 'I won't plant anything that doesn't bear fruit.' But I never agreed with her. For me, the fruit, the reward of gardening, is the beauty. It's the trees. It's the shade. It's the flowers that feed the soul. I like the old saying of the English, 'If you have two shillings in your pocket, you should use one to buy a loaf of bread, and one to buy a flower.'

"When I was sixteen, I had some flower seeds I wanted to plant in the garden, and my mother wouldn't let me. My Aunt Valitha was there that afternoon, and she wrote me a letter when she got back home that evening."

Dear Marian,

I've been thinking about your garden. I think flowers are important in a garden. And I'm sure your mother agrees. She not only planted the productive seed in her five gardens (her five children), such as obedience and cleanliness. She also planted the seeds of beauty that produce the kindness, consideration, love, the desire to be pleasant, cheerful and a cooperative person. These are the flowers that make life beautiful.

In our gardens we might think of vegetables as the necessities of life, food, clothing and shelter. And we can consider the flowers as those little things so necessary to develop a well-rounded personality. Your mother planted only a few seeds, and it is up to each individual to become beautiful depending on the soil and weather.

We need the dark days and rain for the garden. When the sun appears again, all things seem brighter and so refreshed. There are times we wonder if the sun will ever come through, but it hasn't failed yet. Your mother has five lovely gardens. She has planted out many flowers, and I'm sure she feels the love that has taken root to make the gardens more beautiful than they would be without flowers.

Love,

Aunt Valitha

PS. I'm coming Thursday night and will have some kohlrabi plants.

Since her Aunt Valitha wrote that letter, Marian has starred on the Readlyn High girls' basketball team, earned an M.B.A. at Mankato State University in Minnesota, and headed a food-development team for Bird's Eye, a division of General Foods. But she hasn't changed. Although she has acquired expertise in all areas of horticulture—trees and shrubs, fruits and vegetables—flowers are still the focus of her garden. And she is always combing garage sales for vases in which to offer visitors one cut rose as a memento of the Waseca acreage. "Now, when it's gardening time, the first thing that comes to my mind is radishes, onions, lettuce and tomatoes," Larry said. "For Marian, it's petunias, marigolds, impatiens."

Today, the Fischers' tulip bed has exploded from thirty to twelve hundred bulbs, and their iris collection stretches twenty by fifty feet. Altogether they have three thousand square feet in flower beds, including a formal rose garden with 130 bushes. "The rose garden's all Larry's fault. Originally, we had about fifteen roses planted up at the house. They didn't do very well and I wanted to throw them out. That's me. When something doesn't go right, just get rid of it. But Larry wouldn't let me do that. He said, 'Let's try them by the barn. It's drier and maybe they'll grow better there.' So I

moved only about three of them, and they did so well, we decided we should turn the whole area into a rose garden."

In February, Marian starts her flower and vegetable seedlings, nearly seven hundred in all, in the basement under grow lights—petunia, marigold, tomato, cauliflower, cabbage, Brussels sprout, broccoli and parsley seeds dropped in trays in a soilless mix called Redi-Earth. When the seedlings are small, Marian keeps the lights very close, then as the plants mature, she raises the bulbs up on their metal chains. After a few weeks, she carries the seedlings upstairs to enjoy the natural light of the living room window, then outside to the cold frame, and finally to the garden.

"The secret to successful seedlings is timing. We all learn the same way and make the same mistakes. A gardener using grow lights for the first time will have tomato plants ten inches tall by the first of April, a month and a half too early to set them out."

A tunnel leads from the basement to the root cellar where the Fischers consummate the gardening cycle. One fall when Andrew was only eight months old, Larry dug out the room himself, excavating for weeks until ten-thirty at night, Andrew wrapped in a snowsuit beside him. "I'd work eight hours in town, then eight at home, with a few hours of sleep. And since we'd decided to build a garage, while we were at it we built a root cellar underneath."

"That's our motto—'while we're at it,'" Marian said.

The root cellar was cool, the concrete-block walls damp, the air awash with mold. Pea rock covered the floor and Ball jars stared out from the shelves—beets, green beans and tomatoes afloat in water tinged with their own juices. Quarts and quarts of "Fischer Morning Tonic"—tomato juice laced with parsley, celery and herbs—filled one corner, while twenty-five pounds of carrots lay on its side in another, holes punched in its plastic bag, air circulating up through the wire shelving beneath. On another rack, specially outfitted antique lids clamped down on jars of chicken from the annual slaughter, the yellow skin pressed against the glass.

Because it is below ground, the root cellar is weather-proof, the temperature never climbing above 60 degrees in the summer nor falling below 35 to 40 in the winter. The pea rock on the floor keeps the atmosphere moist and ensures the tubers—carrots, turnips and potatoes—a safe overwintering environment. The Fischers have had carrots last even more than a year, and they regularly store their geraniums in the root cellar, retiring them in October, then bringing out the dormant plants and watering them again in April.

The root cellar is the largest of the Fischers' recent projects. Next, they plan to build tennis courts over the old feed lot. For ten years, they tried resurrecting the lot by creating a fruit orchard, but the soil was so high in nitrogen from the manure that the trees became more susceptible to and eventually died of fire blight. Larry and Marian planted three installments of saplings, and each time the blight, caused by a bacterium which is activated by wet weather, eventually leveled the orchard.

Now, the Fischers have already graded the area for the tennis court and have constructed a retaining wall. Soon, they plan to blacktop. Marian laughs at Larry when he fantasizes about the project. "We don't even play tennis. It's just that Larry can hardly wait to put up trellises. He's got it all figured out. Instead of steel poles, he's going to use six-by-six treated wooden ones, twelve feet tall. Then he wants to plant vines all around, bittersweet for sure, and most likely make a perennial garden in that little sunken area where we have the sundial now."

Fantasies like the tennis court are not new to Larry. He began dreaming about living in the country as a boy when he spent summers at his Aunt Lilly's. "Until I was twelve, she and my uncle had a farm down by Audubon, Iowa, and I'd visit for the summer. I loved going there. My uncle was an old-fashioned farmer with horses. And Aunt Lilly gardened a lot, too. Because of them, I decided that one day I was going to buy a place in the country."

After the tennis court, there will be other projects, for both Larry and Marian are dreamers. Inspired by their childhoods, by their families, by the soil, flowers, trees and vegetables growing around them, they create change as well as continuity in their lives. When they open their family album, black-and-white shots of the old tumble-down farm are affixed next to a page of color prints of the renovated house—new porch, enlarged kitchen and living room with a nest of bay windows, and the rebuilt barn, both structures painted red against a bank of snow. In another print, the new three-car garage is receiving its last coat of red, and, already framed in, the attic is on its way to becoming quarters for a full-time gardener to help the Fischers in their old age.

For now, Larry and Marian don't need to hire help. Rather, when they relax in their living room over coffee at five-thiry in the morning, they thumb through catalogues to choose the variety of bittersweet for the tennis court trellises, or settle on the date for the next chicken kill, or sketch a design for protective netting to cover the black raspberries. They smile and remember how each year Aunt Lilly picks the berries just a little too red. But that's one of the reasons Aunt Lilly comes to visit, and that's why the berries are there.

# 4  The Blessing of the Fields

I really feel that if everyone would go back to nature and experience its joys, we wouldn't have to worry about people putting razor blades in candy. A lot of vandalism and crime is the result of boredom. I'm thinking of the street kids in the big cities who "hang around" with nothing to do. I'm also thinking of people in this area who have nothing better to do than go to the corner tavern and drink beer and shoot pool. I'm also thinking of the white-collar crowd who loves to go have a "couple of drinks" at a nice bar, waste a whole Saturday night at a cocktail party, or a whole Sunday watching ball games. You don't find gardeners doing these things. Or even wanting to do them. For gardeners there is so little time in life, so much to do and enjoy. For gardeners, there is no time to waste!—JENNIFER TRAPP, *Salem, Wisconsin*

I've had quite a time with my asparagus bed over the years, but it's beginning to do things I want it to. I always liked asparagus, and I couldn't afford it from the store. So I thought, I ought to be able to grow that! I just think I'll try. So I bought five crowns, dug a big trench, and planted the asparagus. The roots had little tentacles and were silly-looking. They seemed dead. But they all came up. Then one year, it was exceedingly wet and I lost all but two crowns. I thought, Well, that won't do me. So I replaced those with five new crowns. But every time there was a heavy rain that spring, the asparagus struggled. Finally I brought in dirt and raised the beds so the water would run off the sides. And it worked! This year I had five good weeks of cutting. For me gardening takes a certain amount of courage. Just going in there and replanting isn't easy. It fascinates me that things will grow, then die, then grow again. I don't know why I grow plants, but I'm very grateful that I can.

—HELEN WESTON, *Topeka, Kansas*


My wife, Jean, says we're going to have to cut the garden back next year. Only commercial people raise this much. And I don't garden commercially. I do it strictly for friends. But the garden does take a lot of time. It takes a week to plant everything. And then some days we pick as many as fifty to sixty melons. Sometimes I come out here and pick for half a day. But I raise everything for the fun of it. And I give most of it away. I took an early retirement. I'm afflicted with diabetes, so I have the time. I drive around town and give melons to friends. And then I've got a brother up in the Cities, so I take a pickup full of watermelon and muskmelon and meet him halfway in Owatonna. Later I do the same with squash. And then we have a daughter in Winona, and we give her vegetables, too. We can't cover everybody, but we do the best we can.

—DR. LEROY NELSON, *Bricelyn, Minnesota*


You know, my knees and legs were bothering me so bad this winter, I told everybody, "I'm not going to garden anymore. I just can't get around." And then, by the time spring came around, by gosh, by golly, I felt so good I just had to get out there. And I did—every morning at five o'clock. I hated to make myself a liar, but I just couldn't keep away.—IRA ERICSON, *Bishop Hill, Illinois*

# The Blessing of
# the Fields

An Interview with

Father James Henderson

*I was born in Saint Paul, Minnesota, in 1931, and attended*

*Saint Thomas College (we lived only a block from there), gradu-*

*ating with a B.A. in English literature in 1953. That fall, I*

*entered New Melleray Abbey and have been here ever since—*

*except for several years helping out in one of our Trappist mon-*

*asteries outside Winnipeg, Canada, and eight years in Rhode*

*Island working with the Charismatic Renewal Movement. I*

*have been gardening at New Melleray for eight years, beginning*

*with a small herb plot, and gradually expanding to the present*

*"spread." I had only dabbled in gardening in Saint Paul, but it*

*was just enough to catch the bug. Each year is a new experi-*

*ence—finding my own limits of time and energy, as well as*

*experimenting with new varieties and methods.*

*—Father James Henderson, Dubuque, Iowa*

W e rocked and bounced over the weedy lane that twisted through thirty-five hundred acres of corn and soybeans. The three of us were squeezed into the cab of the truck, Father James Henderson, the gardener at New Melleray Abbey near Dubuque, Iowa, pressed against the door, his arm crooked out the window. In the rearview mirror the abbey's image followed us, the three-story limestone castle-like building commanding its position from atop the highest hill. A stretch of grass and pine trees, stations of the cross nailed to their trunks, flowed away from the abbey, and large white Adirondack chairs dotted the lawn where a monk in sandals and a black-and-white cassock visited with retreatants.

For a century, agriculture and gardening have been the primary means of support of the Trappist monks at this abbey hidden among the rolling hills near the Mississippi River. Founded in the twelfth century, the order is one of total seclusion, with the monk's day divided into a rhythm of prayer, religious study, meditation and work, most often manual labor. The monks rise at three A.M. and speak only when necessary, spending their first six hours in Mass, matins and morning prayer. Several times a day, they regroup for office, prime, terce, sext, none, vespers and compline, but the heart of the daylight hours is devoted to work—everything from farming and bookbinding to cleaning.

*Mew-ew-ew. Mew-ew-ew.* The sound filled the cab.

"What was that?" We scanned the road for a cat, afraid we might catch it under our wheels.

"That was me," Father Jim smiled. "We have catbirds here in the garden and I like to call them. I was pulling weeds one morning and imitated the catbird's call. I got it to come up close to me, just two or three feet away. As I'm gardening, I imitate the birds. And that's how I discovered the hummingbirds have a little call like the sparrow's. *Tseet, tseet.* If you listen, the birds teach you their songs."

Father Jim grew up in Saint Paul and joined the Trappists right after college in 1953. He has been at New Melleray ever since but for a decade-long charismatic quest during the 1970s when he was called to leave the monastery—though he remained active in the church—and sojourned along the East Coast. Upon his return to the abbey in the early eighties, Father Jim asked to garden, and ever since he began his first small plot of herbs, he has approached nature with a serenity that calls to mind Saint

*Father James Henderson*

Francis of Assisi. For most people, gardening is an attempt to tame the wilderness and a constant battle against drought, quack grass, grasshoppers, or groundhogs. Father Jim hasn't been without his adversaries, but he meets them with a gentleness that allows him entry into their world. Nature teaches him, and as much as he can, he cooperates.

"Now turn down the hill here, and I'll show you our garden." At a fork in the road, Father Jim pointed toward the left and we drove through a tunnel of corn, the stalks rising six feet into the air, crowding over us on either side of the truck, their tassels bright yellow against the sky. Father Jim reached into his back pocket for a bandanna and, pulling off his golf hat, his gray hair ringed and wet underneath, he blotted his forehead, then removed his wire-rimmed glasses and dabbed his eyes. His face was wide, ruddy, his fine, straight nose the most prominent feature. Several ballpoint pens poked out of his plaid shirt, which, neatly buttoned and a bit tight around the stomach, hung over his blue slacks. The cuffs flared around his Birkenstock sandals.

A small bee flew in the window and buzzed our ears. We swatted it away. "Those are sweat bees, attracted to perspiration. They won't hurt you. They don't really have much of a bite, more like a mosquito." The bee circled around the steering wheel and out the opposite window. "Now, just down at the bottom of the lane here, drive on out through that field. But I'm warning you, you're going to be engulfed by weeds in the garden."

The springs of the truck creaked as we veered off the lane and up the grassy rise toward the plot. Buttonweed and lamb's-quarter, burdock and thistle pinged against the grill, sending small grasshoppers and white cabbage butterflies winging up into the windshield. Then, Father Jim's five-acre garden appeared below, one acre just of herbs in raised beds, the other four in one-hundred-foot-long rows of vegetables that sloped gently away from us.

At the top of the hill, a chimney from a greenhouse stretched up into the air and mimicked the shape of the cross mounted over the gate of the graveyard two hundred feet to the south. Weeds sprouted everywhere: up and through the squash vines, through the strawberry bed, between the hills of sweet corn and green beans. A row of asparagus paralleled the graveyard fence, the frilly tips of the plants peeking out of the quack grass.

"I told you there were weeds. I was picking asparagus this summer and threw my back out. Then I got the flu and that took another week off. And then—this is crazy—a couple of days after that, I was lifting some real heavy rocks and did it the wrong way, like a stupid idiot. I know how to do it right because I used to work in the quarry here at the abbey when we were building on the addition in 1953. Now, with all these weeds, I'm like someone who missed the bus and is running down the street trying to catch it. And I haven't caught it yet!

"But I've got one principle that I follow. People keep trying to tell me it's the wrong principle, but I'm still using it anyway. That is: Plant more than you'll be able to care for. And then if you have time, it's neat. And if you don't, well, it's all right, too."

The midafternoon sun shone hot on our backs, the mosquitoes landing on our necks, biting our ankles. Swarms of gnats hung in the air, and as we passed through their dark clouds, the insects clung to our arms and rode along with us. We slapped and hit at the bugs while Father Jim, untouched, steered us through the weeds, his sandals crunching along the path.

"When I was a small child in Saint Paul, there was a woman at the end of the block who had a fabulous garden. Sometimes I'd sneak up and smell things. Finally, she came out one day and started talking to me. She must have been in her eighties and was so willing to share her time, which was unusual, because, more often, if we kids got into anybody's yard, we'd get the opposite reaction. My encounter with that old woman was the beginning of my love for gardening.

"Yet my own gardening experience didn't begin until I returned from my quest. I started the quest not knowing where I was going and ended up in a prayer house in Rhode Island where I began a little garden. But it was the story of my life. Because we were always going off giving retreats, the plot turned to weeds.

"Then I met a retired couple in Massachusetts who taught me how to control weeds with mulch. They had mulched for so many years that their garden was about a foot higher than the yard. It was like stepping on a sponge, so nice and soft. I learned an awful lot from that couple. And when I came back to New Melleray, I decided I wanted to garden for real. But here, I had to sneak into gardening."

Since the house already had a gardening monk when Father Jim returned to New Melleray, he went back to his previous job in the bookbindery. But he was eventually given permission to start a small herb garden, then a little parsnip patch. The following year the abbey gardener, a hermit who lived in the woods four days a week and had limited time, asked Father Jim if he wanted to expand his plot. "Then like the elephant who got his nose in the tent, my garden got bigger and bigger!

"Originally, I had been attracted to the Trappists because they were a farming order. I was a city boy who wanted to farm. Very romantic. But I was assigned to the bookbindery, which is a nice craft, too. Yet, when I returned from my quest, I wanted to be out in the fresh air. And today, if I weren't working in the garden, I might not even be working on the farm at all because they don't need that much help any more. We have forty-two monks in the house and the people they need for the farm are primarily those who can run the large combines. See, we used to have a dairy herd, beef cattle, purebred Angus, and chickens. But now, it's 'Get big or get out!' So, at this moment, we have corn, corn, corn.

"But our house is the only one in the U.S.—and we have twelve in the States—that can still make its way primarily with agriculture. And New Melleray's success isn't due as much to its size as to its soil. A monastery in Georgia has such poor soil that they've gone into other things. Jellies. And Gethsemani has cheeses and fruitcakes.

"But let me show you something we do grow here that the monks really like. This year I bought parsnip seeds but didn't have time to get them in. When I do, we not only boil and roast the parsnips, but use them as a coffee substitute. The guys like it so much that most of the parsnips go as a beverage now. Some of the monks thought the parsnips would taste like coffee. But they have a flavor all of their own. It's more like a real good Postum."

Father Jim headed down several more rows, these long with hilled-up mounds of sweet potato vines sprawling in all directions. A straw mulch covered both sides of the mounds with black plastic visible underneath on the south. Because the monks had tried before to grow sweet potatoes without success, Father Jim at first believed that he couldn't grow them at the abbey. But one of the sisters from the nearby Trappestine convent who had been raising the root crop for years taught him her secret: mounding and mulching the plants.

"The mulch heats up the soil, and according to my sister friend, sweet potatoes love the heat. But the mound is what's important. If you just put the seedlings in the flat ground, the roots keep going, instead of bulging and making a potato. The sister puts black plastic on both sides of her mound, but because I have a limited budget, I just bought enough plastic to go on the south. You wouldn't believe how warm it stays in the mound. One cold day this summer, I was pulling weeds in the sweet potatoes, and I could feel the warmth coming up from beneath the plastic."

A wren called from somewhere behind us. *Chatter-burble-chatter.* We whirled around, and spotted Father Jim at the end of the row, hands folded together at his waist, his lips pursed. "I've enlisted the wrens to help me in the greenhouse. Would you like to see it?"

Parting the weeds, we wandered through a grove of pine trees and rested for a moment in the shade on an old hay wagon, four or five flats of seedlings scattered on the bed: begonias, pansies, salvia and phlox. A monarch butterfly landed on a milkweed blossom, fanning its wings open to the sun, while tree frogs hopped out of the goldenrod. *Chatter-burble-chatter.* Father Jim whistled, and patted his forehead with his bandanna. Perspiration dribbled down our faces, our chests, our underarms and backs, the sun beaming through the gauzy layer of cloud cover.

The greenhouse, a 10 × 20-foot building with eight windows in the roof propped open for ventilation, was surrounded by giant sunflowers, their heads drooping with seeds, many of the outer leaves on the stems beginning to dry and curl under. Beds of petunias, dark purple and pink trumpets, blossomed at the door, and inside, a thermometer read 110 degrees— 20 degrees hotter than outdoors. The dirt floor of the greenhouse was planted entirely in tomatoes, the long vines tied up to pipes mounted from ceiling rafters. A worn flannel workshirt was draped over one of the pipes next to the furnace. A snakeskin coiled near its base.

"When fuel prices were cheap, we heated the greenhouse in the winter and began all our plants from seed in flats set out along the tables that run the length of the building. But now, in early spring, I get two bookcases without backs and put them up to the window sills in my cell inside the abbey. Then I put the flats on the bookshelves. Last year I expanded and got another shelf with three grow lights, and this year I went berserk with three more."

In late March, Father Jim transplants the seedlings into the greenhouse, where he keeps their lower leaves trimmed off to help promote air circulation and counteract fungus growth. "And there's another little tip I've learned. Every once in awhile I'd go out to the muskmelon patch and notice

a vine completely limp, dead. The fungus had killed it. But it took me two years to figure out what I was doing. See, first I'd come in here and check the tomatoes, then I'd go out and rummage around to see if there were any melons ripe on the vines. I was transferring the fungus from the tomatoes to the muskmelons. And since I stopped doing that, I haven't had any problems.

"They say, too, that people who smoke should wash their hands before they work with tomatoes because tobacco plants have the same kind of disease as tomatoes. Tobacco and tomato plants are in the same family—nightshade. You transfer the disease on your fingers and even your work-pants. So, now I actually have two pairs of bib overalls that I wear, one for the morning when I do the tomatoes and one for the afternoon when I do the rest of the vegetables.

"And I had another problem. I was having trouble with the tomato horn-worms in here. Then I started imitating the wrens when I was working in the greenhouse. I whistled them in, and from then on I didn't have a single hornworm! And then the birds started coming on their own. The first year I gardened, I only went into the greenhouse in the afternoons, but one day I went in the morning. The wrens were in here, and boy, did they give me a hard time. You know, they were chattering so. Then I silently made an agreement with them that I would come to the greenhouse only in the afternoons. And as long as I keep my word, I don't find any hornworms. Unfortunately, the wren's one of the first birds to leave in the fall, and then I begin to see worms again."

Wrens weren't the only wildlife in the greenhouse. Father Jim encourages garter snakes to crawl through the dirt and eat mice, which chew on the tomatoes, and he feels the snakes provide a better control than poison. "I hate to put anything like D-Con around because it could contaminate what we eat. And we intentionally let wasps nest around the ceiling pipes because they consume a lot of pests. People come in and out and the wasps never bother them, so what the heck!"

Father Jim took off his glasses and wiped the perspiration from his eyes, then he leaned back against a potting table, the tomato vines spiraling above his head toward the ceiling, pushing out the roof window. His shirt still looked cool and freshly laundered as he folded his arms across his chest. His face, clear of emotion, was almost translucent.

"The previous greenhouse gardener was an old monk from Ireland, and he showed me how to tie up tomatoes." Father Jim pointed at the ground, a string anchored firmly in the dirt near the roots of a tomato plant, the other end tied to one of the pipes near the ceiling. With his index finger, he traced the path of the string through the air. "The old priest didn't tie the string real tight but left it loose so that the tomato stem could expand and twirl as it grew up all the way to the ceiling. The strings are better supports than stakes, and you can tie new ones for all the suckers.

"The old priest taught me never to prune the suckers. I'd read that you always do that. But he went against the books and said, 'Just watch. That's where your tomatoes are going to come from.' Sure enough, it's the suckers that give millions of tomatoes.

"And I remember another crazy little tip from that monk. He was a nervous, jerky sort of person. And when he'd move around the tomatoes, sometimes he'd break off a stem. If it was one that he wanted to save, he put a Band-Aid around where it was broken. And within a week, that stem would knit!"

Picking up a long garden hose, Father Jim turned on a faucet under the potting table. Slowly, water trickled from the nozzle and onto the dirt floor. He tested its temperature, the water dribbling over his hands and off the ends of his fingers. "Our water is taken from the last uncontaminated aquifer in the United States. We have a very, very deep well." He tipped the nozzle upwards and offered us a drink.

Outside, the 90 degree air was almost refreshing. On the south side of the greenhouse, Father Jim had planted a flower garden, with phlox, lily of the valley, cosmos, peonies, snapdragons and salvia at our feet, hollyhocks—bright red, pink and yellow—at eye level. Beyond the garden, the white limestone abbey bell tower spired above the trees. Down the hill again, sparrows twittered in the pine grove and a cardinal whistled shrilly.

"There's one of my little friends. *What-cheer, cheer, cheer*," Father Jim answered.

In the herb garden, we meandered between raised beds along paths covered with newspaper, a mulching technique Father Jim had learned from the retired Massachusetts couple. "I use the paper between the raised beds to keep the weeds down and help with absorption. Even in the hardest rain, the soil never runs off. I don't use the comic section or anything highly colored because there's too much lead in the ink."

Extra bails of newspaper were bound with twine and scattered around the path, five or six clumps stacked together and swallowed up in the weeds. Father Jim laughed and motioned us away. "One day I was coming up to pull weeds around those stacks and I heard this little *meow* sound. And it wasn't a cat. It wasn't even a catbird. No, it was a skunk. Since then, I've been keeping away. That's why those weeds have just been left."

Hesitating, Father Jim stopped to watch the cardinal land on a hollyhock near us. It cocked its head to the side, one eye scanning the garden. Father Jim broke off tiny leaves from several herbs, then held them to his nose. "Know what this is? People always think it's pineapple mint, but it isn't. It's apple mint. I dry it and combine it with peppermint to make a tea for the retreatants in the guesthouse. They love it. And this is tansy. I dry the flowers and save them for Christmas wreaths. Too, tansy is supposed to be a fly repellant. The early settlers planted it at their kitchen door to keep the flies from the house, but I see flies on it all the time."

Rummaging on the ground for another weed, Father Jim rose with a piece of purslane. "Did you ever hear that fish oil is real good for cholesterol? They've discovered that this plant has the same ingredient as fish oil. Really, some of the plants we consider weeds are more nutritious than the things we cultivate. How about amaranth, or pigweed? There's another weed

we hoe out all the time. Amaranth is very high in vitamins. And do you know what's really nice steamed? Stinging nettle. It has an even nicer flavor than spinach and contains silica, which is good for your heart."

Soon we found ourselves in a large strawberry patch, masses of low-lying plants stretching fifty feet. Father Jim had wanted enough berries to make jam for the whole community, so had ordered 250 new plants that spring. "But I waited and waited and the darn things didn't come. I had the plot all tilled and ready. So, I figured they weren't going to come and I put buckwheat in that spot. Then one day in one of our walk-in coolers I discovered the box of strawberries. I don't know who got the box, but I think he took it for granted that I'd see them in the freezer."

The old priest who had been in charge of the greenhouse had also cultivated strawberries and had taught Father Jim to turn under the plants every two years to eradicate a root fungus. "He said if you keep tilling below the rows like that, and keep changing the plants, the fungus doesn't get a head start. So, after the strawberries bear, I till under the first four rows, and the runners from the new plants fill in the space."

It was four-fifteen, forty-five minutes before vespers, the sun moving farther west in the sky but still glowing hot, and Father Jim wanted to show us the rest of the grounds. On the way back to the truck, he cupped a tiny flower in his hand, curling his body toward it, his nose close to its white trumpet-shaped blossom.

"This year, for the first time, I started smelling bindweed flowers, and I couldn't believe it. They're like white water lilies or like custard, with a strong, spicy smell." He snapped off several leaves from another mintlike herb. Popping one into his mouth, he passed us each a sprig.

"It's lemon balm," Father Jim said, walking over a series of large, evenly spaced limestone slabs. "I had planned to make a path with these stones and had half of the slabs down. This area was clear last year. But this summer, the balm spread so, I didn't have the heart to rip it out. So, this year I moved the stones and am beginning the path again, to route it around the lemon balm."

In the truck, we squeezed together again, three in the cab. We passed the old dairy barn. A small shed next to it had served as a chapel for the monks who said office there after early morning milking. Further up the road, Father Jim pointed out a sawmill and carpenter's shop, then a chicken coop that was being insulated for use as a hermitage. "The coop was on sale, made from redwood by mistake. We bought it for less than half price. And soon we'll take it out to the woods. The brothers drink from a little stream out there and usually come back to the main house once a week to stock up on food. One of the permanent hermits has deliberately simplified his meals and eats mostly peanut butter sandwiches."

We jiggled and bucked up another hill and were surrounded by fifty apple trees, deep crevices in their bark, branches heavy with red fruit just ripening. With his elbow out the window, Father Jim motioned us back toward the abbey. The sun cast a pink glow on its blond walls. We skirted an open prairie which had once been used as pasture to graze the order's cattle, but when the monks sold their herd, they seeded the expanse with natural grasses and wildflowers. Down the road, a limestone church nestled in the trees, and behind the church the old white stone slabs of a cemetery jutted out of the ground, leaning into each other.

"Every year we come up here and have the blessing of the fields. We have vespers, then a little picnic supper."

We clicked off the ignition and sat awhile in the shade of larch trees. The conifers towered up and around the church, a small breeze just beginning to move their needles. The sun arced away on the horizon, and the evening air was a few degrees cooler. The sparrows had quieted, their silence filled by the hollow sound of the mourning doves.

"We have the largest European larch in Iowa. In the community's early days, a man imported a huge load of them from Russia. He thought many of them would die en route, but most survived. So he donated several to us.

"Gardening is a beautiful exchange. And gardeners, in general, are such good people. While I was called away from the abbey those years, I learned so much from others about gardening and the world. And whenever I have a chance, I try to learn more. I have clogged vertebral arteries and go to a clinic for chelation therapy. An old lady who has had gangrene in her foot also goes there. They had to amputate. They couldn't help it.

"Well, she and her husband live on a farm, and she had always kept a big garden until she lost her foot. But every time we see each other, we talk gardens. And a couple of my rows of muskmelons are from her seeds. She and her husband finally came up with a muskmelon they liked and they saved the seeds and sent me some.

"One of the things she said she missed the most about gardening was not being able to pull weeds. And before I gardened, you know, I wouldn't have understood that, but I can now. It's kind of fun, pulling weeds. It's so peaceful."

The New Melleray bell, throaty and resonant, announced vespers. From all over the monastery—the cornfields, carpenter's shop, sawmill, kitchen, laundry and library—monks disappeared into the chapel, their hoods down, black-and-white cassocks brushing their sandals. Father Jim tugged open the truck door handle. Outside, he leaned into the window and lingered for awhile as he said good-bye. *Bong, bong.* "That's the final bell." Father Jim turned away.

Minutes later, the Adirondack chairs empty, the pink glow on the abbey walls turning blue, forty-two male voices rose in chant: Lord have mercy . . . Christ have mercy . . . Lord have mercy . . . My help is in the name of the Lord who hath made heaven and earth.

# Gardening and the God Within

## An Interview with Carl Birkelbach

*I was born on the west side of Chicago, an only child of Polish-German parents, and shared a bedroom with my Polish grandmother. During World War II, she had a Victory garden, and although I did not speak much Polish, we communicated very deeply about vegetables. I graduated from Bradley University in 1962, and am now the president of Birkelbach Investment Securities, and the author of* Stock Market Profits through Charting. *I am a frequent guest on CBS television news, and have my own weekly television program, "The Stock Market Observer," which airs on local Chicago stations. Every weekend I leave the city behind to enjoy the fresh air of Trevor, Wisconsin, where I have a large vegetable garden and wildlife sanctuary.*

*—Carl Birkelbach, Trevor, Wisconsin*

C arl Birkelbach has to drive for an hour and a half to cultivate his garden—all the way from his investment business in Chicago's Loop to his weekend home in Trevor, Wisconsin. Every Friday at three-thirty he scoops up his two identically marked black-and-white-mongrel dogs, Lucky and Koo, then inches northward in his Blazer along Lake Shore Drive through the rush-hour traffic, past the Pick Congress Hotel, the Sears Tower and the Marina high-rise apartments.

"I equate my Friday drive to quantum analysis. Each car is like an electron, holding me back, holding me in. Around four-thirty as I get through the traffic and near the Wisconsin border, my spirits begin to break loose. I wonder which of the wildflowers I've planted will be in bloom this week, whether any of the tomatoes will be red, and if I'll see my woodpecker. I even imagine myself sitting at my kitchen table with a cup of coffee, looking off along my prairie and the two hundred fruit trees I've planted to the marsh in the distance.

"Coming to my farm helps ground me in my spirituality. I went to college in the sixties, to Bradley University, and had, shall we say, a good time. Then after an early marriage, two daughters, divorce, and business highs and lows, I became more contemplative. But I haven't given up worldly pleasures as did Thomas Merton, whose poetry and theology I often read on the weekends up here. He became a hermit within a Trappist order at Our Lady of Gethsemani monastery in Kentucky."

Short, muscular, with a fringe of hair circling his balding head, Carl speaks with a broad Chicago accent, pronouncing his "a's" as diphthongs and punctuating his phrases by the lifting and dropping of his voice. As he straddled the antique pine chair in the kitchen of his Wisconsin sanctuary, he epitomized the young executive, his polo shirt and blue cotton shorts the perfect leisure attire. A cathedral ceiling opened above him, and on the room's white walls hung an assemblage of rural antiques: cowbells, snowshoes, an ox yoke, a handwoven basket, a seed planter, a level, a square. An old wooden scythe filled one corner of the room like a Calder sculpture, and in another a ten-gallon pickling crock displayed an arrangement of cornstalks and dried prairie grasses.

But this scene with its *Country Living* glossiness is misleading, for Carl is full of contradictions. He is worldly and cosmopolitan, yet as he scooted his chair closer to the long wooden table, he looked elfish, his movements staccato, his smile broad enough to reveal a sparkle from one of his molars.

He is jovial yet nervous, grinning while at the same time digging his index finger into the quick of his thumbnail. Even Carl's apparent image of physical well-being is undercut by the missing tip of his nose and the jagged scar running down the right side of his face from his ear to the base of his neck—vestiges of a pet dog attack when Carl was fourteen years old.

And these contradictions penetrate beyond the physical. Carl is at the same time a spiritualist and a materialist. He is a loner and an extrovert, capable of spending a weekend in solitude in Wisconsin, then driving home Sunday night to celebrate Chicago's Polish Days with a beer bash at a friend's apartment. He is both analytical and intuitive, a stockbroker in love with the glamour and calculations of high finance as well as a gardener who longs to be outdoors digging, plowing, weeding, landscaping and actively meditating on his place in nature.

"I spend my weeks constantly involved with money and the workings of the world. As a broker, you have to know what's going on politically and socially because world events affect the economy which in turn affects investments. Stocks, bonds, interest rates, inflation rates, gold prices are all tied together and I need to be on top of them every market day. But on Friday afternoon, I leave the ticker tape behind, and come up here where I think of my house and land as my sanctuary."

The route Carl takes to his refuge winds through a tangle of small Wisconsin towns. Some are resorts fronting lakes, the streets crammed with restaurants and gift shops, the sidewalks crowded with vacationers in bermudas and Topsiders. Others still belong to the locals, and in these towns pickup trucks and motorcycles nose together in front of lounges like the Badger, the Moonlight and the Red Velvet. Near Trevor, Carl passes a small lake, one of dozens in the area, where plush modern homes and trailer parks, fancy country inns and beer joints compete for space around its rim.

"My biggest fear is that they're going to put a mobile home park next to my property. We're halfway between Chicago and Milwaukee, so we appreciate the open space we have. As I turn down this last gravel road, the other cars are gone. And I begin to fly. It's a great psychological release coming up here to my garden, a spiritual feeling of safety."

At five o'clock when Carl arrives at his forty acres, he unlocks the thousand-pound double-jack padlocked chain that secures the gate across the drive. A grove of bur oaks, shagbark hickories and full-sized firs Carl had trucked in from a neighboring nursery screen a one-story ranch house and a barn. Shooting up waist high, prairie flowers and grasses stretch from the road to the gravel drive, and border the 30 × 60-foot vegetable garden, then spread out toward the fruit orchard and marsh.

Carl parks his Blazer in the barn out of sight of the three-tiered deck he built on the back of the house. "Once I get up here and am relaxing in my hammock, I don't want to see a single car." Then he unlocks the double deadbolts of his front door, disconnects the burglar alarm (installed after his third break-in), and within fifteen minutes is outside running his rototiller down the wide rows of his vegetables.

"When I come up here to Wisconsin on the weekends, the first thing I do is take care of my garden. I've always felt a latent need for gardening which I can trace back to my Polish grandmother. Bushia lived with us and she and I were very close. She couldn't speak much English and I couldn't speak much Polish, but we seemed to communicate very well together."

Carl's grandmother was literally born in the fields of Poland. When she was in her twenties, she immigrated to Milwaukee and married Carl's grandfather, who worked in the steel mills. After the grandfather's early death, Bushia earned a living as a cleaning woman on Chicago's Lake Shore Drive in a high-rise similar to the building Carl lives in now.

"When I was small my family rented the upstairs of a house. The land-lady had an immaculate lawn, and we weren't allowed to play on the grass. But during World War II, with her son in the army and President Roosevelt coming out and saying that the way you could support the war effort was through planting a garden, the landlady told us we could till a plot. My grandmother was all excited. But I had no idea about gardening.

"I remember once, something really mysterious happened. In those days they still had rag collectors, junk collectors and some fruit vendors who would go through the alley with horses and wagons. My grandmother and I were out in the garden one day when one of those peddlers came by. The horse let go, and I thought, Oooh, ugh. But my grandmother got the shovel and went over there and picked up the manure and put it in the garden.

"I didn't know what Bushia was doing. But I talked to my mother later and she said, 'Haven't you noticed? There are horses all over the city, and the streets are always clean!' Everyone used the manure in their gardens. The gardeners actually cleaned the streets," Carl laughed, leaning over to the Mr. Coffee machine on the counter and refilling his mug. He stirred in a teaspoon of sugar and, before taking a sip, blew on the liquid to cool it.

"My grandmother spent a lot of time in the garden. I think she felt a connection to the ground. I imagine you're a little lonesome in a foreign country, and yet when you're planting in the earth, you feel at home. But my mother didn't garden. It's interesting. When you come from an agricul-tural society as my grandmother did—at that time a peasant was one step above a serf—the next generation arrives in America to make the American dream come true. And one of the things you may not want to do is get your hands dirty.

"I remember my mother making apple pies with the fruit we had from our trees when my parents finally bought a home in Brookfield, Illinois. That was delightful! But my mother didn't want to get into the ground at all. So, in my family, it's from dirty hands to dirty hands in three generations."

Today, Carl unites his grandmother's connection to the earth and his mother's aspirations for upward mobility. Even his acreage incorporates the two poles. Carl safeguards the ecology of the marsh and savanna that stretches for twenty acres from his deck and relishes their profusion of wildlife: the herons, sandhill cranes, cattails and dragonflies. But he also ceaselessly upgrades his house, and has refurbished everything from the shingle roof to the forged-iron coat hooks in the mud room. Even the kitchen table bears Carl's imprint.

"See, this table came from a nunnery. Each nun had her own place and kept her silverware and napkin here." Carl yanked open one of the twelve drawers. "When I bought this at the antique store, the top was covered with oilcloth. But I pulled that up and put on these oak tongue-and-groove boards. Then I refinished and stained the whole thing."

But even before transforming the house, Carl created his garden. "Trying to find a place for the plot was difficult. I wanted it close to the house but not too close. And I wanted it close to a water source, which becomes very important in the kind of season we've been running through lately. Now, there used to be a railroad bed that ran straight through this place because there were gravel pits in Wilmot, nearby. I found that the place where I wanted to put my garden was a good six inches deep in gravel. But being very determined, I took my spade and dug.

"With each wheelbarrowful, I moved more of that unsuitable environment. And you know, I belong to an athletic club, and I'll go work out pumping iron and jogging and getting sweaty. But this was manual labor for a purpose. I could feel every muscle I used to dig out this garden. Shovelful by shovelful, for one whole year, I dug.

"I worked through 90 degree temperatures in the summer, and during the fall and spring I often worked through the rain. Yes, it was hard work. And yes, I was getting dirty, but my body was just singing! And every Friday on my drive up, my mind would lift as the traffic started to expand and I could drive a little faster."

With the same energy, Carl built his deck, trucked in trees and hung wren houses and feeders from their branches. He fashioned shutters for the house windows and flooded window boxes with red, white and pink petunias, with geraniums and ferns. Inside, he reconstructed what had once been a dark kitchen and formal dining room into a sunny country kitchen. "I knocked out the wall, pulled up the linoleum floor and put down oak tongue-and-groove boards again. Then I steamed off the wallpaper, which was covered with little roses."

Rising at five-thirty A.M., Carl worked twelve- to fourteen-hour days. And he worked with a vision. "I tried to create my sanctuary according to Frank Lloyd Wright's precepts where your entire ecological space is an organic whole. I took a new tract house—orange with black trim—whose design was diametrically opposed to its landscape, and made it look old, painting it and the barn the same beige-gray color to blend in with the environment.

"The whole acreage had been farmed and used as a horse pasture, the grass overgrazed and the earth worn out and packed down. I rototilled and planted to counteract erosion and let things go back to a more natural state." Carl paused and in the glare of an early July morning watched Koo as she bounded off the deck toward the marsh.

The tiny dog disappeared in the prairie grass streaked with coneflowers, goldenrod, loosestrife and Queen Anne's lace. Gathered in clumps, the wildflowers dotted the savanna—purple, yellow, fuchsia, white—standing perfectly still in the hot sun. A small creek meandered along one side of the expanse, and elm, oak and willow trees clung to its banks, the willow's branches flowing down to meet the grasses. On the other side of the savanna, a mowed path cut through the prairie and opened a triangle for a baseball diamond, its bases worn spots, then pushed on toward an orchard of apples, plums and pears.

Lucky, the older and slower of the two dogs, remained on the deck. Disabled from a stroke, Lucky cocked his head to one side, his small ears flopping over, eyes slightly bulged, right leg dragging. "Last winter Lucky had an attack of kidney stones and the vet thought I'd have to put him down. But all night long I prayed that the stones would pass. I stayed up and prayed over and over again to Saint Jude. And do you know what? Thank you, Saint Jude. In the morning, the stones passed!

"Lucky's a city dog. I found him in an alley down by Wrigley Field in Chicago, and he reminded me of a little mutt I had when I was growing up. That dog was named Lucky, also. So, this guy here is Lucky II. When I bought the place, Lucky was scared of the outdoors. He always wanted to be close to the house. One night he got brave, though, and went visiting down the road. Several months later the neighbor called up and said his registered cocker spaniel had had a litter of mutts. I went down to see the pups, and there was no doubt who the father was. The puppies all looked just like Lucky. What could I say? I took the female home and named her Kochanie. That's Polish for 'loved one.' But I call her Koo for short."

Carl clicked the fan in the kitchen from "Low" to "Medium," then turned back to us. "I'm happy to have Koo now that Lucky's getting so old I'm up nights praying for his life. Of course, Lucky isn't the only reason I pray."

*Koo*

In 1974, Carl had split off from the brokerage firm where he worked to start his own business. Not afraid of risk, he gambled on a flamboyant organizational plan leasing offices in a new, prime location and leasing out space to other brokers. Soon Carl's business was solvent and started to grow.

"Arriving at my new plan required introspection, changing from one side of my brain to the other, and I did most of my thinking up here while gardening. I was risking capital. I'd broken up with my woman friend, and didn't know what the next step was going to be. But this sanctuary is my strength."

Carl flicked his head toward the sliding glass doors, then suddenly pushed up from the table and dashed into a room off the kitchen, returning with a pair of binoculars and a Roger Tory Peterson *Field Guide to the Birds.* Peering off into the marsh, he focused on a great blue heron, then passed the binoculars to us. "Can you see him?" Carl danced at the window and pointed to the bird, its wings spread four feet wide, feathers a darker blue-grey at the tips, neck pulled into an S, legs trailing behind its body. The heron glided closer toward us, then vanished above the house.

"Herons, squirrels, rabbits, deer and a red fox. I have all sorts of friends here, and they have a spot where they can feel safe. I've seen sandhill cranes on their migrations. Just the other day, I had a red-headed woodpecker that died, and I felt like I'd lost a friend. I dug a hole and buried him."

For Carl, all wildlife at his acreage is sacred, and he works to protect an environment where nature can thrive. He traces his commitment to the land back to the late sixties, when eighteen-year-olds were drafted into the Vietnam War yet did not have the vote, when we were destroying a people and a country without actually knowing why. "During the war, America began rethinking its values. For the first time we started questioning our government and the flag. Bobby Kennedy and Martin Luther King were assassinated, and there were riots. That was the period when we had the Democratic convention in Chicago with Mayor Daley. It was a very moving time.

"And one of the issues I began thinking about then was the environment. That was the first time we realized that animals were becoming extinct, that we were poisoning our soil and air. I remember reading Rachel Carson's *Silent Spring.* When the book came out, we felt the beginning of the environmental movement, but it never really filtered into the general thought of the masses until 1967."

During the time of the Vietnam War, Carl became a vegetarian, and his diet led him to think about gardening and owning land. He read *Living the Good Life* by Helen and Scott Nearing, a couple who left New York City to homestead in Vermont. "They were some of the first people who saw problems with the environment and decided that they wanted to become independent of our mechanized society. The Nearings rebuilt an old farm and started an organic garden, working half a day on the land and using the other half for their crafts and enjoyment. And they were able to do it! Along with the help of maple syrup, which brought in some good solid cash."

After absorbing the Nearings' book, Carl studied herbs and began jogging. "I remember the first time I ran a mile, I thought it was so exciting. In those days, people used to see me along Lake Michigan and wonder what I was running from! Of course, at this same time I owned a hot dog stand. That's right, we served tacos, hot dogs and hamburgers. The contradiction never bothered me. I was still a vegetarian. After about a year and a half, though, I began working my way back to meat. I'm still careful about what I eat and consume a lot of vegetables. But every now and then, a steak looks awfully good!

"Hold on a second." A fly swooped toward Carl's coffee cup, and he whacked at it with his *Field Guide*. Then he grabbed the swatter from the mud room and chased the insect around the table and into the living room, where it landed on the round window Carl had installed to give him a view of the bird feeder he had built and hung among the hickories. "Got him! In the country, you *do* have insects." Carl laughed, a deep, hearty chuckle, and tugged off his shirt.

The morning temperatures were rising into the eighties and Koo panted for water. Lucky flopped down on the deck outside in a cool spot in the shade of a planter. He yawned, his mouth opening to reveal his few remaining teeth, yellow and chipped, while Koo trotted into the house and slurped at her water bowl.

Carl slid through the glass doors, then across the deck and over the gravel driveway to his garden. A large fenced plot, sheltered between the house and the barn, the garden mirrored Carl's personality. Viewed from a distance, it appeared tranquil and orderly, straight wide rows of vegetables running up and down the sixty-foot length, the area between the rows cultivated and clean. Closer up, with large zucchini plants dominating, their leaves fanning out over the black dirt, the garden hinted at exuberance. Carrots, lettuce, onions, red and green cabbage swelled out of the soil while tangles of beans wound up around strings anchored to a center pole to form a teepee. Side shoots of broccoli poked out from thick main stems, some of them already bursting into delicate yellow flowers. The air was piquant with mint, the south edge of the plot overrun with its spear-shaped leaves.

Carl leaned against the fence, his arms brushing the railing next to the bird feeder. "See how wide my rows are? With all my vegetables and flowers, I'd be doing nothing but picking weeds. So, I plant far enough apart to run a rototiller through. I can just get that thing going, *brrrrrrr*, and in about ten minutes I'm finished.

"Yes, I have weeds all over the place. This garden is incredibly fertile. And that goes back to my Bushia. After I dug out my garden plot, I began filling it in. My neighbor, who has a landscape business, was excavating a pond, and he had the machinery to bring the dirt over. I spread it by hand. Then another friend had horses and I got a truckload of manure and dumped it and mixed the peat and manure together. So, I imitated Bushia, and it was a great start. I was really excited!

"But I soon learned there's a problem with manure. It's full of weed seed. My first year was absolutely horrendous for weeds. That's the year my daughters decided they never wanted to garden again. So the dirty hands are skipping another generation."

Carl stooped over and picked a dandelion, then brushed a mosquito off his arm.

"Since bringing in the manure, I've been working compost and mixing it into the garden. Once you have good soil, you don't have much trouble with insects and blight. That way you can avoid pesticides. Another way to avoid sprays is simply to grow the vegetables that do well in your location. Zucchini, butternut squash, tomatoes, pole beans all love it here, while lima beans do not. I plant romaine lettuce because it gets hot in June and all the other lettuces taste bitter.

"Oh, and I also planted some mint. That does well. Too well! One sprig, and now all of Kenosha County is full of it. There's no way I can pick all that. But I do try to keep the garden as clean as possible. Of course, there's really nothing I can do about weeds overtaking the flowers in my prairie."

Carl gestured toward the expanse of land that circled his house, and began strolling along a path that headed toward the marsh. The sun beamed straight above. Carl slapped at a mosquito on his shoulder and yanked his shirt back over his head, tucking the tail into his shorts. Lucky hobbled beside him, tongue out, dangling at a slant from his pitched head, while Koo darted after a ground squirrel.

The seed heads of prairie grasses and flowers brushed against Carl's waist as the white tip of Koo's tail disappeared into a thicket of compass plants. Tall members of the sunflower family and indigenous to Wisconsin, the plants rose six feet in the air and were splattered with bright yellow daisy-like flowers.

"As soon as I got my vegetable garden going, I tilled up the whole front lawn and bought a thousand dollars' worth of wildflower seeds and grasses. And that thousand dollars only got me a pailful of seeds, so I spread it all very carefully by hand in the spring when the rains would keep the ground moist. It's important to keep the seeds wet. I raked them in about an inch deep and stomped them into the ground. When things started coming up on a regular basis, I found that certain flowers would blossom all at once, one color dominating for a while, then another. For instance, in the spring, the white daisies are thick, then there's the purple loosestrife, the black-eyed Susans, then later in the summer the white Queen Anne's lace. And soon we're going to have goldenrod!

"But one of these days I'm going to have to decide if I want trees or wildflowers. The oaks and hickories are so close to the prairie, their seeds have taken hold in some places. And the only real way to eradicate trees is to burn. Prairie fires served that purpose in the old days. But I've hesitated to burn off the prairie because my house is so close. Of course, out toward the marsh, I've worked for a couple of years planting trees—at least a thousand pines and fifty fruit trees. I take long walks around my place, my pruning shears in my back pocket."

Carl sauntered on past young apple trees, their trunks wound with brown-paper wrap to guard against grazing deer and rabbits, toward pear, peach and cherry trees. It was just before noon, the sky beginning to cloud over, the humidity higher. Koo rolled in a spot by the creek.

"Let me give you a pruning demonstration," Carl said, pointing to a young pear. The tree, a Stark Spur from Stark Brothers, was a semi-dwarf and would grow twelve to fifteen feet. With more spurs than normal on

each limb, it bears from the trunk outward, doubling the production of the fruit. "When these trees arrive in the mail, they look like yardsticks and you need to keep the roots cooled off. You can think of it like a burn. That's the way these roots feel when they're out of water, or dry."

With the tips of his pruning shears, Carl traced each of the three branches coming off the main trunk of the pear tree. "You look for a couple of the biggest branches to leaf out, and leave only those, cutting them back just three or four inches from the base of the trunk. So it really doesn't look like you're planting very much to begin with."

Part of the art of pruning is to facilitate picking, and Carl crops the tops of some of his pears to force the trees to grow horizontally, lower to the ground, making the fruit easier to reach. But most important, he prunes to thin out the weak branches, making certain the tree is compact and strong, able to bear up under the weight of the fruit.

"There's all sorts of ways to prune, but the important thing is that when you make your cut, you make it just above the bud. Don't go too far in. Don't go too far out."

Carl came to a cluster of purple coneflowers, their black seedheads raised and rounded, eyes staring up, the spiked petals falling away at the base. Carl crouched in the flowers, hands braced on thighs, head peeking over the flashes of purple, and posed for a photograph. "Zucchini!" He drew out the final *eeee* sound and the shutter clicked.

"I talk about dirty hands to dirty hands in three generations. And I joke about my daughters rejecting gardening. But when you're young, you tend to rebel against your parents' values. Yet simply because you're exposed to your parents' interests, the values remain with you. I see my children learning from me, whether it's classical music or an appreciation for nature. Just being around the garden and seeing me there and knowing how happy I am with it makes an impression on them. When I take my walks here I often think about the future, realizing how important these things are to pass on.

"And I think of gardening from a self-sufficiency point of view. In communist countries, half of the food production comes out of private gardens, and I know that's particularly important in Poland. Even in the United States, growing your own food is one of the ways of gaining financial security. Every week I work at investing money for people. You put a million dollars in the bank and it earns $x$ amount of interest—eight thousand dollars a year, eighty thousand, whatever—that's what we normally think of as financial security. But if for some reason you can't get food with that money, you're going to starve to death. So, life isn't just having money."

For a moment, Carl became pensive, the only sounds the shrill whistle of a cardinal, the chirping of the sparrows, the clink of the dogs' tags. A red-tailed hawk glided overhead, and grasshoppers clung to the little bluestem and prairie dropseed grasses, their large compound eyes holding us in their gaze before the insects flew through the damp air to the next stem. Ahead, Lucky plopped down under an apple tree for a quick rest.

"A theologian I read, Teilhard de Chardin, says that all nature once evolved from a single point of convergence, that time and consciousness came together in a spiritual peak moment. Gardening, at least, tends to extend time, to make it more flowy. One of the things I like best about gardening is just watching the plants grow. No, I mean it. I like watching them develop in their small ways. Plants grow and change as the seasons evolve. You sense a movement, but it's more expansive and isn't broken up into rigid components—weeks and months. It's more one continuum.

"In my garden, I have a feeling of accomplishment and self-fulfillment that you can't get in any other way. It helps me be closer to God, to the

God within myself. Too, you feel you've earned something when you've planted your seed, cultivated it, picked the weeds, picked the plant and cooked it yourself."

Carl neared the house again where early Monday morning, dressed in his three-piece suit, he would bend over the vegetables in his garden with a knife and paper bag, harvesting lettuce, tomatoes and zucchini to take back to the city. Next, he would lock the doors and windows, reset the burglar alarm and head back out the drive, stopping to secure the heavy metal chain around the gate. Then, attaché case full of quarterly reports wedged against the bag of vegetables on the floor of the Blazer, he would bounce down the gravel road toward the tollway to Chicago, one dog in the seat behind staring straight ahead, the other wagging his tail in the back, watching through the rear window as the prairie grass disappeared.

# God's Little Half Acre

## An Interview with Grant Cushinberry

*I was born in Nicodemus, Kansas. That's a black town that was settled by ex-slaves who homesteaded in the Kansas territory. I moved with my parents to Hoisington, Kansas, then served four years in the armed forces as a combat medic. After World War II, I came back to Topeka and attended Washburn University. Then I worked thirty years at the VA hospital. At that time, I started up a garbage collection business and a lawn-mowing service. Now I'm retired, and run a free clothing store, hold an annual free watermelon feed at the Grant Cushinberry Park in Topeka, put on a free Thanksgiving dinner for five thousand people and garden God's Little Half Acre, where people in need come and pick vegetables. I've written a book of poems called* My Stories, *and there is a movie of my life in the making. My love for gardening started back when my father was a farmer and gardening was a way of survival to feed family and neighbors.*

—Grant Cushinberry, Topeka, Kansas

There was no doubt about it. The playful collection of yard decor nearly obscuring the tiny ranch house had to belong to Grant Cushinberry. But Grant didn't seem to be home. Even though his white Cadillac glistened in the driveway, all was silent behind the padlocked grille surrounding the property. Beyond the white wrought-iron front gate stamped with curlicues and flowers and decorated with signs commanding SMILE: IT'S THE SECOND BEST THING YOU CAN DO WITH YOUR LIPS and THIS HOUSE GUARDED BY SHOTGUNS THREE NIGHTS A WEEK: YOU GUESS WHICH NIGHTS, beyond the flamingos, the donkeys and swans on the lawn, and the bottomless painted buckets strung from the front porch, the windows were all sealed, the heavy silence of the Kansas heat wave unbroken by the whir of fans or the buzz of air conditioning.

Suddenly, the growl of an engine charged the air, and a midnight blue Bronco, its doors richly stenciled with gold paint, skidded into the driveway.

"Sorry I'm late. I'm always on the run," Grant said as he sprang from the cab and motioned us to follow him up the block, his yellow AIAW Division Softball Champion T-shirt contouring his muscles, his face slick with perspiration.

Known throughout Topeka as a flamboyant man, Grant earns a living collecting garbage. But his real vocation is giving help and pleasure to others: the Cushinberry Clothing Bank, to which some of the city's finest stores donate items for the needy; an annual Cushinberry parade of antique cars and motorcycles to commemorate the arrival of the Exodusters, ex-slaves who escaped from the South and came to Kansas to homestead; an annual Cushinberry Thanksgiving dinner for over five thousand held in Topeka's Expo Hall; and, every summer for the past fifteen years, "God's Little Half Acre," a garden Grant plants and those in need harvest.

"I was just at a meeting with the city council about that park they named after me. And after this, I got to run over to my church. I'm in charge of the congregate meals there. I clean up afterwards. Otherwise, you know, they drop food all over the floor, and the cockroaches come. And then, I got a meeting about this parade tomorrow. The antique guys want to be in the parade, but they don't want to put their cars on the back because they go too slow and heat up. So, I got to get in touch with the parade master, and tell him to put the antique cars at the top, so that they can drop out."

By now Grant had steered us three houses past his own, around two

*Grant Cushinberry*

garbage trucks, their front bumpers announcing HERE COMES CUSHINBERRY, then across a lawn and behind yet another house into an empty lot crammed with junked stoves, refrigerators, beds, lamps, toilets, sinks, books, paint cans, ladders and, in one corner, a collection of elementary-school-sized desks and chairs.

"See all this?" Grant stopped under a basketball hoop and thrust his muscular hand into the air. His face, the features clean and bold, was in the shadow of the dense foliage of American elms screening the back lot. "I bought out a secondhand store, and then a lot of this come out of some of my rent houses. Next Saturday, I'm gonna haul it all onto that garden up there, you know, God's Little Half Acre, and let people come by and get whatever they want." Grant slid his hands back onto his hips and riveted his eyes on us, his face stone serious, the pencil-thin moustache that descended from each nostril then rode across his upper lip set in a line. A large crease intersected his high, smooth forehead, and his gray hair, cropped short, was beginning to recede.

"I don't have much planted up in the garden now, just some collards and cherry tomatoes. The wind blew the tomatoes over, but I got straw under them to keep them from rotting. And a few okries, and a short row of cabbages. What you see up there is the second growth. I've got some ladies and they come and pick every morning all summer. Different ones around the neighborhood. But you should've seen the place in the spring. I had greens. I had lettuce and onions, beets and cucumbers.

"Now I don't have time. I'm on the run. I've got so many things I do. Do you know about my watermelon feed? Down at my park Sunday? I'm gonna buy a truckload of watermelons. I've been trying to get the best deal I can get. They're still expensive. Eight cents a pound. And last week I had a barbecue down there. Did you read about that in the paper? We barbecued a whole hog. Gave away sandwiches, too."

We had read about Grant's barbecue feed, as well as the antique car parade, in the *Topeka Capitol Journal*. We'd also watched Grant on the "MacNeil/Lehrer Report" that past Thanksgiving Day, when he was interviewed about his annual dinner for five thousand. But in print and on the screen, Grant is flatter, more subdued, than in person, when he emits the steady charge of a man geared up for action. Negotiating, arbitrating, scheduling, arranging, speaking, gardening, you could easily imagine Grant in perpetual motion, calm and determined, but perpetual nonetheless.

"By the time I lay down . . . ," he chuckled. Then his features froze and his expression became stern. "Well, I really can't sleep long. Got too much to do. I usually work in my garden early in the morning, about five o'clock when it's cool. I write at night. Then I can collect my thoughts from the daytime. I can think better at night, too, when I don't got nobody to disturb me. You know, I write three columns, one on the editorial page of the *Topeka Capitol Journal*. Had a big one in there in the Saturday paper, an editorial about alcoholics and drugs and stuff. I write a column for them once a month. And then I got two other black papers I write for. They're weekly papers, but I write for them whenever I find time. And I got a book in the library, too. *Cushinberry Stories*. They're just short incidents that happened to me. I'm in the process of writing another, too, if I can find the time."

That day, Grant was even more pressed than usual. He had just returned from a weekend in his hometown, Nicodemus, Kansas, an all-black community, where he had gone to celebrate the annual Founders' Day Weekend, two days of Ernestine's barbecue, parades and local talent shows. Though now almost defunct (its official population stands at eighty), Nicodemus manages to hold on, coming back to life each July, when four hundred to five hundred relatives of the original settlers arrive to celebrate and commemorate—though this year's attendance had been down because of the heat.

"Yeah, Nicodemus, that's my town. I was born there. But I was raised in Hoisington. I'm from a family of nine, and everybody had to work in the garden to keep us alive. Yeah, I've been gardening ever since I was a kid. But I didn't get God's Little Half Acre going until about fifteen years ago. To begin with, I wanted it to be a community garden. Well, see these goals here? I train a bunch of kids all the time. This here's a basketball court. And back then, we had a track field up there on God's Little Half Acre. So I just turned that into a garden. Then I asked the Neighborhood Improvement Association, the NIA, to help me out. I said to them, 'Why don't you guys help me bear some of the expenses of plowing and all that?' But the NIA come back and said, 'Well, we can't help you because somebody will get hurt and they'll want to sue us.' So I had to take the garden over myself. At first, I just let people come in and I'd tell them, 'You have that plot of ground, ten by four over there. Plant something.' Well, they'd plant something. Then they'd leave it. I'd have to end up taking care of it myself.

People think you can put the seeds in and go. So, I said, 'I'll just do it all by myself.' Then all I got to do is put it in the paper when it's ready. 'Course now, sometimes people'll ask me on the street, 'Is it ready?' 'Why don't you come help me prepare it?' I want to tell them. But I don't."

Grant stopped talking for a moment, his eyes fixing us the way the eyes of a preacher might bore into a congregation. A circle of light reflected off Grant's forehead and funneled down his nose from bridge to tip. His jaw was tight. With one hand braced on his hip, a small scar midway up his forearm reflecting the light, Grant held his stance while an old plastic bag caught under a paint can fluttered beside him in the first hint of morning breeze.

"I'm from a small town and everybody had a garden to make ends meet. Like I told you before, everybody in my family had to work. Folks give you so much ground to take care of and you had to take care. We growed everything but sugar. We used to put a big crop in, and like it gets to hoe time, and you got to hoe them beans. You know, you got to hoe this over here and that over there before you played. We gardened mostly on Saturdays. During the week we went to school and after school you had to cut wood and milk cows.

"On Saturday, the main deal was that we all washed because all the kids was home that day. We had a big pot out and we'd heat the water. My mother and sisters would rub board and they'd clean the clothes. And then, you'd get on one end and wring the wash and hang the clothes on the line. And somebody had to keep the pot rolling real hot. We made our own soap, too. That lye soap. Then after that, we'd clean the barn and the chicken house. And then we'd start working on the garden. When that was done, we could go play. Oh, we always managed to get a little playing time on Saturdays.

"But Sunday, every living soul had to go to church. My mother cooked on Saturday, and when we come in from church, all she had to do was warm that dinner and put it on the table. She didn't allow us to dance or play no music on Sunday. That's the way we was brought up. Had to go to church. She always brought some old preacher home for dinner. We had to be on our best behavior. You giggled, and my mother gave you a glance and you was almost whipped. Boy, my little mother, she was only five-foot-two! My dad was six-foot-seven and weighed over three hundred pounds. He didn't whip us because he'd kill us. His hands was about this big around." Grant raised his own large hands from his hips, fingers splayed to form the outlines of a basketball. The facets of his diamond pinky ring twinkled.

"So my mother did all the disciplines. But boy, she could hit you harder than lightning could bump a stump. We worked from sunup through the day, and my little mother, she didn't have to say but one thing, 'Do this.' And boy, if you didn't do that, you better give your heart to God, because your behind was hers."

Trained by his mother to put in long hours, once he reached Topeka Grant held two jobs for over twenty years, working for the Menninger Clinic by day and the VA hospital at night. He wanted to be certain he earned enough for his children to receive college educations. "But around those mental patients, you know, you listen to their problems and you feel so bad. After a while, I just got me a regular truck and started running the alleys and picking things up. Then I bought a trash route. Then I bought another trash route. In all, I bought six different ones. Then I had a lawn service. I worked half a day on my trash route. Then I'd get to the lawns.

"And I always sponsored a basketball team, too. We'd take the kids just out of high school going into college and get some experience underneath them. See, I got lights here at night. I got benches out here, too." Grant flicked his head toward the other side of the court, then asked if we would like to sit down. Before we could answer, he began navigating through the piles of junk to the two benches, end-to-end along the edge of the dirt, the varnish long worn away, the wood gray and warped.

"See, I got bicycles here, too. I only got about seven or eight now. But I used to collect them in the summertime, then I'd fix them up in the winter and give them to kids for presents. Now I don't got time for that. All spring and summer I work in God's Little Half Acre."

We had passed Grant's garden earlier. With its combination of practicality and whimsy—forty-foot rows of okra and collards, bales of hay rising four feet into the air along an entire side, cherry tomatoes sprawling in another quadrant, all juxtaposed with the sign out front whose bold cornucopia might have been painted by a child, the hot-pink benches flanking the gate, and the electric fan strung onto a post and plugged into nowhere—the garden was clearly the project of a man who liked equal parts of hard work and fun.

It was also the product of a man for whom the scale of life is large. Each

summer Grant plants a quarter of an acre of red and green okra, one of his favorite dishes, which he instructs must be cooked slowly. And he sows his collards in four twenty-foot-long dense rows, then separates and transplants the seedlings later to cover one-half of his entire second-growth summer garden. He complains, though, that people don't harvest the collards correctly. "I keep telling my ladies, 'All you do is pick the leaves.' And when the collards get enough rain on them, you take four big leaves, and that's a mess. Just cook them up with some ham or salt pork, put them on your plate and eat them up. Well, I put vinegar on mine. No mystery to it."

If there is a secret, an elixir, to Grant's gardening, it is hay. All summer long he collects bales which he uses during the growing season as a mulch under his cherry tomatoes. At the end of the summer, when he has harvested the last of his vegetables, he divides the rest of the hay, doling out half of it as winter bedding for pet dogs and cats, then spreading the remainder over his plot. "See, I take the hay loose from the bale before I give it away, 'cause one guy have one cat and he might come and take a whole bale. But if I take it and tear it loose, he's gonna be too lazy to take the whole thing." Then, after the first snowfall, Grant plows the hay under, leaves it for several weeks, and turns it under again. "Plow it the first time with big grooves, and the second time I harrow it."

The finer plowing promotes rotting and allows the hay to hold in more moisture. The key is plowing deeply, at least ten inches, then leaving the garden to settle in over the winter. Because the hay keeps the ground soft, when Grant gets ready to plant in the spring the plot is already tilled, and he can sow his vegetables early, reaping two growths, often even three, off the land every season.

In addition to fertilizing the soil, the hay insulates, warming the ground during the winter and cooling it over the summer. "We get a rain and the hay won't let the water go but so far. Keeps it from sinking too deep. Then the heat comes up like this and you can go out there and feel the ground and it still feels damp. Even with this drought, I've never watered. And I probably never will. I'll just wait for a good rain. And then I'll get out there and throw in some mustard seed."

Grant broadcasts his mustard, waiting for a downpour at the end of the season to pound the tiny yellow seeds into the soil so the birds don't pick them up. A cool-weather crop, these late-sown greens will last well into the fall—even after the first frosts which, rather than destroy the plants, actually tenderize the curly leaves.

"I always get in two plantings of mustard. One in the spring and one in the fall. See, black people eat a lot of greens. That was a staple crop out home there. Most of them greens grow wild on the prairie. Like dock. Wild onions. And lamb's-quarters. And we ate all that stuff. And we'd go out on the creek bank and we got all kinds of blueberries and raspberries. Pears and apples. We canned everything 'cause we had all them girls around us. No, we never went hungry. And every year, we'd kill three hogs and one or two beef.

"And then my mother'd always give to people who didn't have nothing. We lived beside the railroad tracks. And in the old days, a train'd come by and the shack would rock. Well, all the bums would get off the train and come to our house. I think they must've been told there was good eating there. All of us kids and my mother'd always find something good to give them! A lot of black people said, 'Why don't you let those white people go and take care of their own?' My mother'd say, 'One day some of my kids might be out in the world.' So she'd give the bums something to eat and they'd go and tell somebody else, and that person would come by and my mother would feed them. She'd say, 'Hunger don't know no color.'

"My mother and hers was real religious. And boy, they pounded that into us. 'When you can help somebody, help them. That's what God put you here for.' A lot of black people got a hang-up on being black. They say they can't get ahead. My mother'd say, 'That's just a cop-out. God gave you the same kind of brain he gave the white fellow. You just got to put out more. When you go for a job, be the first one there and the last one left.' So I learned that pretty early in life.

"My mother taught me that I don't know but one nation. That's the human race. I help whites and blacks alike. A lot of blacks, they ask me, 'Why you help all those white people? They got places they can go.' I say, 'From above, they all look alike.' A lot of black people think white people get more than they do. I tell them, 'A poor white catches as much hell as a poor black.'"

A smile inched across Grant's face, settling on his lips. Then his eyes grew stern once again, his gaze shuttling back and forth between us. The drooping branches of an elm framed his head. The deeply veined matte leaves contrasted with the tautness and luster of Grant's skin, his face—eyes, nose, cheeks, chin—a solid block. The air vibrated with the hum of cicadas. In the distance, a car screeched to a stop.

"Black and white, they come to my garden at the same time. Problem is, the younger generation these days don't know nothing about no gardens. Gardens are hard work. You can't just throw that seed in. You got to put it in the ground, then take care of it. When the seeds come up, you got to plow around them and loosen that soil. Now I got machines, but back in the days when I was growing up, you had to hoe. You got to walk down the whole side and loosen the soil. If the soil's hard, the seed can't push up. And the water's gonna drain right off, too."

Grant scraped against the cement with a discarded tool handle, perspiration winding from his forehead through his graying sideburns and down his cheeks. The pockets of his pants, the waistband tucked under his belly, jangled with keys. "And you got to keep the weeds out. With all that hay rotting down there, they grow, but they sap the soil. Now, when I was a kid, we used manure to fertilize because we had cattle. One year I remember, we put so much manure on the ground that we burned up all our potatoes. It was hot out there. The weather come down and we didn't get no rain. Just burned the potatoes right into the ground.

"But 'cept for the weather, we didn't have trouble with losing our crops. We didn't need no sprays or scarecrows in those days. No, we had BB guns and we had chickens and guineas. They chased everything off. Yup, guin-

eas, they sit up in the tree and swoop down on everything. Chicken hawks'd be flying around up there and the guineas'd give the warning to our chickens and they'd head for our lumber. We always kept our lumber high. The old chicken hawk wouldn't go underneath that. He'd go way out in a flat field, just swoop down and pick them chickens up. But guineas see him coming and they'd start screaming. Just like a woman. *Eeeeech, eeeeech.* Yeah, my family knows how to garden. We've been doing it for centuries."

In the late 1870s Grant's great-grandparents, along with other ex-slaves from Kentucky and Tennessee, traveled north to settle in Kansas. There they created towns named Rattlebone Hollow, Juniper, Wyandotte City, and Graverstown, where Grant's relatives carved out their homestead. The first winter was hard. The immigrants arrived too late in the season to break sod and plant crops, so many of the men had to go to work for the Kansas Pacific Railroad. They acquired the name Exodusters, and they sang songs as they worked, extolling Kansas as the land that gave them freedom. Over the next several years the Exodusters labored to establish black farming colonies, with more and more blacks immigrating until the movement reached a flood in 1879, when between fifteen and twenty thousand blacks arrived in Kansas during a four-month period. The influx caused backlash and overcrowding, and within several years two-thirds of the immigrants had left the state, their farm colonies eventually dying out. Grant's family stayed.

"My grandparents and great-grandparents, they gardened. From one generation to another, they tell how all the horses died, and my great-granddad, he hooked up a milk cow and he plowed a lot of acres with her. One kid went along and shooed the flies off, and another one led the cow, and another kid held the plow. Yes, sirree, they plowed acres and acres with that cow. And then, in the evening time, they milked her." Grant chuckled. Then his eyes froze, the whites laced with minute red veins.

"And one of my uncles, or some relation—he lived down in the South then—he did something in town and the Klan come out to whup him. My auntie was pregnant and she got in between them. About ten or twelve guys was there to beat him. So, she just stood in the way, and they knocked her in the head and hung her up by the heels. They cut the baby out of her stomach and it just fell to the ground. Then my uncle, he said, 'Let me go into the house and get a blanket to cover my wife.' The Klan said, 'Go ahead. We going to kill him when he get back anyway.' So, he went in and got his gun and shot five of them. Then he ran all day and all night until he got to Kansas. A few years ago, one of his daughters, an old lady about eighty-five, told me the tale. 'Our name is Cushinberry, but we changed it to Miller, so they couldn't trace him.'

"You know, I talk to different groups, and they say, 'You ought to really be bitter, the way the white folks did to yours.' 'Why should I?' I ask them. 'I wasn't there. Why should I keep hatred in my heart for something your grandparents did against mine? We got to let everybody live and make this a better world.' And one of the ways we make this world better is by working.

"When I was a kid, if we didn't work, we didn't eat. If you didn't grow a big garden, winter'd come along and you'd be in trouble. We had cellars then, none of that modern stuff like deep freezes. We'd put everything in jars and kill our own beef, and we had a smokehouse. We had wheat and we took it to the granary and they'd grind that wheat up and put it in barrels. And we kept that all down in our cellar. Be real cool, like air conditioning. You know, they got a big mound of dirt and that dirt acts just like insulation. The moisture from the bottom keeps it cool.

"Like in my great-grandparents' sod house. It was cool in there, but it was full of snakes. We always kept a little dog in the house to kill the snakes. There was a lot of rattlers out there. They'd drop right down from the ceiling. Those dogs, they'd see a snake crawling around and they'd kill it. A snake'll bite a dog and it won't bother them. Bite a horse and it'll kill them. That's why we worked mules. Mules won't walk in a hole. Horse fall in a hole and he'll break his ankles and you got to shoot him. But a mule'll shy around that hole.

"My parents had all kinds of mules and horses. And I used to herd cows along the railroad tracks. My job was to keep them off the tracks if the trains was coming. Some of those cows, about time for milking, they get on that track and want to go home. You had to shoo them off. So you couldn't be laying around under the shade tree. You had to stay on the horse, and you always had a whip. You'd get up and whack them on the rear. You take that whip and just pop it. Sounded just like a shotgun. You get them cows like that across the rear and they'll get the picture.

"But now there ain't anybody left in the town where I grew up. See, in the smaller towns after World War II, if your folks didn't own some property or some business, they just got up and left because there wasn't no work. Seven hundred people, that was the whole population when I left. The railroad evaporated. That's what most of the people worked for. My daddy worked for them, too. He come to the depot and picked the trains up. Then he'd take them to the roundhouse and he'd clean them up and put water in them and put coal in that chute. He'd pull the chute down and he'd fill up that bin, then he'd take it around and fill that big tank with water. Then he'd wash that train off and bring it back around on the tracks. He could ride that train as well as any engineer, but they wouldn't let blacks do that. Only thing they let blacks do on the railroad was fix the tracks and be a porter."

Grant hopped to his feet and stood on the edge of the basketball court, his hands braced on his hips. His T-shirt was drawn tight across his beefy chest. Underneath his running shoes the cement was cracked and pocked, the basketball court spread out around him, a concrete garden sprouting castoffs: on his left, a set of waterlogged children's encyclopedias, behind him a toilet, a ring of rust etched into the bowl, and on his right a pile of curtain rods.

"My father worked hard. Everybody did in them days. Yeah, I was used to hard work. Back then we had these big old cement carts called the Georgia buggy. We'd start at one end paving the whole block. There'd be two iron wheels and sixteen hundred pounds of cement. Two of you had to push that sixteen hundred pounds, and you had to push even. If one pushed too hard, the thing would roll around. Teamwork. You'd run from the hopper clear down to the other end. And when you got to the other end, you just let it loose and turned it over. You dropped that concrete. You poured it out and started back down and loaded up again. We worked ten hours back in them days. Yeah, I been used to hard work from the day I was born.

"As soon as you hit the floor, you had to be in the garden. Nobody'd be in the house. So you had to go right along with the family. At first, they'd probably just put me under the tree. But everybody had something to do. And back in them days, you didn't argue. When they told you what to do, you did it. My kids, they'd argue. 'Why do I have to do this?' And you'd have to set down and explain it. You try to be a little bit modern. My folks just said, 'You do it.'

"And I still work hard today. For twenty years I could only get three or four hours of sleep. Then it just became natural. I wake up at five-thirty in the morning and I wonder why I'm getting up so early. That's when I work in the garden."

Grant steered us back across the vacant lot, past his trash truck decorated with a handpainted mural of Topeka, the downtown and capitol buildings springing up from an island surrounded by white-capped water dotted with sailboats. Out front, the sidewalks were deserted. The heat rose from the street in steamy waves, the asphalt shiny with humidity. None of the usual neighborhood noises, no dogs, no children, no screen doors, orchestrated the day—the only sound the whir of cicadas, which grew more intense as we approached the open land of God's Little Half Acre. "See those sunflowers up there in the shape of a T? The T's for Topeka. It's art. Yard art, I call it."

On the old church bulletin sign in front of the garden, Grant had created additional yard art: his own version of a cornucopia, a bowl mounded with brightly colored fruits and vegetables—corn, squash, tomatoes and watermelon—with the words "God's Little Half Acre" lettered above on a background of gold and red chevrons and the assurance "God Loves You!" below.

We sat down on the benches, the yellow corrugated roof overhead blocking the intense sun. Grant pointed to the far end of his garden where

white and purple okra blossoms nodded under umbrella-shaped leaves. "That okrie likes the hot August weather, but you got to pick it before it gets too big. City folks don't know how to pick vegetables like country folks do. If you ask me, all around, the country is a better place to grow up than the city. You get more insight on human nature. In the city, everybody pass you by like a freight train pass a hobo. They ain't got time. I had a problem when I first come to the city. I waved at everybody. It just comes naturally. And you say, 'Good morning.' Once I went out and told a lady, 'Good morning.' 'You know me?' she asked. 'No, I just said, "Good morning."'"

Grant laughed, breaking into a huge grin, his sloping shoulders jiggling. For the first time that afternoon, his body relaxed, hands falling open at his sides, jaw slack. All sternness had vanished from his face. Suddenly he looked boyish. A 1975 Plymouth Volare coasted by. Grant waved to the driver, then looked down at his watch. "I got to be going now. Sorry I can't show you around the rest of the garden. I got to run off to the congregate meal, then I got to go meet with the city council. And I still got to get this parade set for tomorrow. All I do is run. But I do it for the love of helping people. Once an old guy told me no matter what you do in life, how big a funeral you have is gonna depend on the weather. But I don't live by that. I still take my money and spend it on others. I don't want to be the richest man in the graveyard. I want to spread mine around."

Grant gripped the edge of the wooden bench and checked his watch again, then shifted his weight to the balls of his feet. Once more the air was charged with energy as he prepared to set himself in motion. "I got wounded twice overseas, and when I was laying over there in a foxhole, I told the good Lord if he let me survive, I wanted to dedicate my life to helping those less fortunate. And let me tell you, it's a good warm feeling to lay down at night and think you've helped somebody."

# Other Bur Oak Books

*A Cook's Tour of Iowa*
By Susan Puckett

*Fragile Giants: A Natural History of the Loess Hills*
By Cornelia F. Mutel

*More han Ola og han Per*
By Peter J. Rosendahl

*Old Capitol: Portrait of an Iowa Landmark*
By Margaret N. Keyes

*A Place of Sense: Essays in Search of the Midwest*
Edited by Michael Martone

*A Ruth Suckow Omnibus*
By Ruth Suckow

*"A Secret to Be Burried": The Diary and Life of Emily Hawley Gillespie, 1858–1888*
By Judy Nolte Lensink

*Tales of an Old Horsetrader: The First Hundred Years*
By Leroy Judson Daniels

*The Tattooed Countess*
By Carl Van Vechten

*Vandemark's Folly*
By Herbert Quick

7576　　　　4191